My Heart is a Golden Buddha

My Heart is a Golden Buddha
Buddhist Stories from Korea

First Edition: September, 2006
Third Edition: October, 2012
Fourth Edition: May, 2014

© 2014 Hanmaum Seonwon Foundation
All rights reserved, including the right to reproduce this work in any form.

English translation and editing by
Hanmaum International Culture Institute

Cover Design by Su Yeon Park

Hanmaum Publications
www.hanmaumbooks.com
tel: (82-31)470-3175 / fax: (82-31)470-3209
E-mail: onemind@hanmaum.org

ISBN 978-89-91857-27-8 (03220)

Buddhist Stories from Korea

My Heart Is A Golden Buddha

Seon Master Daehaeng

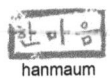
hanmaum

Table of Contents

Foreword	*6*
Introduction	*10*
About Daehaeng Kun Sunim	*13*
1. The Four Wives	*16*
2. Dog Meat and the Seon Master	*22*
3. A Greedy Daughter-in-law	*26*
4. Red Bean Porridge	*32*
5. Making a Mirror	*40*
6. Parents' Endless Love	*44*
7. The Man Who Ran Out of Merit	*54*
8. The General's Strange Dream	*60*
9. The Fox that Fell in a Hole	*64*
10. The Man who Became a Cow	*68*
11. Ananda and the Keyhole	*74*
12. Worm Soup	*80*
13. Buckwheat Dumplings	*86*
14. Wonhyo's Awakening	*92*
15. Wisdom Guides the Way	*96*

16.	Letting Go	*102*
17.	Like a Centipede	*108*
18.	All by Yourself	*112*
19.	Three Grains of Millet	*118*
20.	The Same Dream	*124*
21.	The Good for Nothing Son	*130*
22.	The Travels of a Seon Master	*136*
23.	Even a Tree Understands Gratitude	*144*
24.	The Pure-hearted Sculptor	*148*
25.	The Scholar and the Regent	*156*
26.	Bodhidharma's Sandal	*162*
27.	It's Hard to Say	*168*
28.	Mother-in-law Saves the Family	*172*
29.	The Man with Two Sets of Parents	*178*
30.	The King and the Blacksmith	*184*
31.	The Examination	*190*
32.	Carrying a Sheep on Your Shoulders	*198*
33.	True Giving	*204*

Foreword

When the first edition of this beautiful little book, *My Heart is a Golden Buddha*, by one of Korea's foremost Seon Masters, the nun Daehaeng Kun Sunim, was delivered to me in New York, its size and shape fit comfortably in the palm of my hand as if it belonged here. It brought to mind a "Book of Hours," one of those famous little works calligraphed and illustrated by hand in medieval European monasteries in the days before printing. They were small, precious books that people kept close to them and read over and over again as portable prayer books.

Reading this book, I was reminded of the wondrous medieval Japanese story collections I discovered as a graduate student. These were stories about kings and generals, bandits and monks, and poor farmers. And there were also salt-makers, nuns, soldiers, scholars, fishermen, ladies of the court, star-crossed lovers, and elderly couples praying for the birth of a longed-for child. They contained the whole panorama of life on earth. There were even stories about the longings and needs of plants and animals, told as if there were no distinctions between them and human beings. Scholars mistook these for children's tales, but like the present stories, they were actually windows into the dilemmas and liberation of the human heart.

One collection I was particularly fond of had eventually been printed by wood-block in the 17th century under the title of *Otogi-zōshi* (御伽草子). The title is difficult to translate, but it means something like "stories that will keep you company." I loved this title. It was as if the stories were to function as a parent leading a child, or a nurse lending comfort and strength to one weak in body, or a spiritual master guiding one who feels lost or who wavers. The miraculous power of faith and the astonishing strength that can emerge from the human heart in life and across lifetimes was evident everywhere in these stories. Whenever one felt in need of direction, comfort, or guidance, the collection was waiting at one's elbow, a silent companion, ready to shed light.

Now, here in the 21st century, Daehaeng Kun Sunim has continued this tradition with down-to-earth stories about simple, recognizable people doing all manner of everyday interesting things, yet rich with wisdom that emanates from the depths of Korean Buddhist culture. Each tale, though seemingly short and simple, suddenly and unexpectedly releases dammed up perceptions and allows the free flow of resolutions to timeless problems that all earth's inhabitants face. When we pick up this book we may imagine ourselves to be alone, in search of the key to life's problems. Yet as we read her words, story after story, our essential being seems to well up and flow, and we perceive our true natures to be one with the river of the universe.

My Heart is a Golden Buddha is in the true sense a companion book, easy to be with, both fun and comforting, to read again and again to keep one company on the path of life as one seeks first to find, and then to let go. Seon Master Daehaeng's words fall like rain, fill our ears; and fish dance and sing. All readers, young and old, can feel the golden light of the Buddha spreading over them as it shines from her Buddha heart.

These stories resonate beyond Korea and across the world. They are wonderful bedtime reading, parents to child; and wonderful morning reading with that first quiet cup of tea or coffee before the full day ahead; and wonderful to read in old age on quiet, reflective, late afternoons.

One mind, across all ages, all cultures, all generations, all species, across time, glowing golden like a Buddha.

Barbara Ruch
Professor Emeritus, Columbia University
Director of the Institute for
Medieval Japanese Studies

Introduction

The stories collected here were told by Seon Master Daehaeng over the course of forty years of Dharma talks. To everyone listening, most of these tales and their themes would have been familiar. But even when telling a well-known or funny story, she would explain much deeper elements that most people wouldn't have noticed in previous hearings.

Through the foibles of a rich man, she explains the working of the karmic echoes that our actions and thoughts have created. In the misadventures of a monk who went to China to find a teacher, she shows us how to take everything that comes up in our lives as our spiritual practice. And in the story of a poor widow, she explains the infinite power of the fundamental Buddha nature that we all share.

This idea of a foundation we all share, our Buddha nature, is a frequent theme in Seon Master Daehaeng's stories. This foundation is the basis of our connection to all other beings, and the source from which everything arises. And yet this idea is not always easy to understand or accept.

So, in these stories, Seon Master Daehaeng engagingly explains one aspect or nuance after another, until at last we begin to have a sense of what she is talking about. This is the point where things get interesting, for the essence of all spiritual practice lies not in the understanding, but in the application.

Even if you understand only one thing, she urges her students, do your best to consistently put it into practice. Then, that aspect will grow, and as it does, related aspects will naturally become clear to you. As you continue to do this, wisdom and energy will begin to flow forth like cool spring water.

It is our hope that everyone will discover this for themselves!

With palms together,
Hanmaum International Culture Institute
August, 2012

*How can words possibly express our gratitude
for how much your wisdom and compassion
have meant to us?
We'll take what you taught us and put it
into practice through our daily lives.
Sharing it with all we meet, we'll strive to become a blessing
to all around us.*

About Daehaeng Kun Sunim

Daehaeng Kun Sunim(1927-2012)[1] was a rare teacher in Korea: a female seon(zen)[2] master, a nun whose students included monks as well as nuns, and a teacher who helped revitalize Korean Buddhism by dramatically increasing the participation of young people and men.

She broke out of traditional models of spiritual practice to teach in such a way that allowed anyone to practice and awaken, making laypeople a particular focus of her efforts. At the same time, she was a major force for the advancement of Bhikkunis (nuns), heavily supporting traditional nuns' colleges as well as the modern Bhikkuni Council of Korea.

---

1. **Sunim / Kun Sunim:** Sunim is the respectful title of address for a Buddhist monk or nun in Korea, and Kun Sunim is the title given to outstanding nuns or monks.

2. **Seon** (Chan, Zen): Seon describes the unshakeable state where one has firm faith in their inherent foundation, their Buddha-nature, and so returns everything they encounter back to this fundamental mind. It also means letting go of "I," "me," and "mine" throughout one's daily life.

Born in Seoul, Korea, she awakened when she was around eight years old and spent the years that followed learning to put her understanding into practice.

For years, she wandered the mountains of Korea, wearing ragged clothes and eating only what was at hand. Later, she explained that she hadn't been pursuing some type of asceticism; rather, she was just completely absorbed in entrusting everything to her fundamental Buddha essence and observing how that affected her life.

Those years profoundly shaped Kun Sunim's later teaching style; she intimately knew the great potential, energy, and wisdom inherent within each of us, and recognized that most of the people she encountered suffered because they didn't realize this about themselves.

Seeing clearly the great light in every individual, she taught people to rely upon this inherent foundation, and refused to teach anything that distracted from this most important truth.

Her deep compassion made her a legend in Korea long before she formally started teaching. She was known for having the spiritual power to help people in all circumstances with every kind of problem. She compared compassion to freeing a fish from a drying puddle, putting a homeless family into a home, or providing the school fees that would allow a student to finish high school. And when she did things like this, and much more, few knew that she was behind it.

Kun Sunim saw that for people to live freely and go forward in the world as a blessing to all around them, they needed to know about this bright essence that is within each of us.

To help people discover this for themselves, she founded the first Hanmaum Seon Center in 1972 and began to teach. For forty years she gave wisdom to those who needed wisdom, food and money to those who were poor and hungry, and compassion to those who were hurting.

1. The Four Wives

Once upon a time there was a rich man who had four wives. He lacked for nothing, and over the years he had become very comfortable with his life.

However, a day came when the doctors told him he had only a few months to live. He went here and there looking for cures, but they were all useless. It finally began to sink in that he was truly about to die, and the thought terrified him.

Unable to stand the thought of being alone, he sent for his fourth wife, the youngest and prettiest.

"You're the one I love above all the others. You're who I think of first when I'm coming home, and you're who I work so hard for. I worry so much about you when you are ill, and when you get up at night, I can't fall asleep until you've returned. When I die, will you come with me?"

His fourth wife said, "I'll go with you, but only to the edge of your grave."

Disappointed by this, the man called for his third wife. "Sweetie, in order for you to be my wife, I went through so many hardships. The difficulties and tears I had to endure in order to make you mine! If you think about how much I love you, won't you agree to come with me?"

But his third wife replied, "It was you who chased me; I never chased after you, and I'm not going to start now. Once your coffin goes through the front gate, we're done."

Shaken by his third wife's answer, he looked for some comfort from his second wife. "Honey, during all the years we've been together, I've taken good care of you, haven't I? I gave you nice clothes for each season, and whatever you wanted to eat I provided. Didn't I always try to ensure that you were comfortable? Now I don't have much time left and I'm scared. When I die, will you come with me and keep me company?"

Before he even finished, his second wife was shaking her head from side to side. "Are you kidding me? There's no way I'm going with you."

Finally, he asked for his first wife, and spoke to her with a sad, heavy voice. "I'm so sorry that I never paid much attention to you. But we spent many years together, living side by side. Will you go with me to the next world?"

To his astonishment, his first wife said, "Of course I will. I don't care whether you were a good husband or not. Considering all the years we've spent together, how could I not accompany you?"

⁎⁎⁎

In this story, the fourth wife represents family members, such as your children and spouse. You love them so much that you will go without sleep and endure hunger to ensure that they are comfortable and have enough to eat; yet they can go with you only as far your grave.

The third wife stands for money and power. People expend so much effort and go through so many hardships in order to obtain wealth and position. Many will even sacrifice their health and their families for these, yet when death comes, all of their power is useless and they can't take even a single penny with them.

The second wife represents our body. We pour so much effort into taking care of it. We feed it when it's hungry, keep it warm when the weather's cold, and cool it off when it's too hot. But no matter how hard we work at taking care of our body, it won't follow us when we die.

The first wife represents karmic consciousnesses. Even after we take leave of our bodies, these will follow us. As we go through life, each action and state of mind, both good and bad, is recorded within us one by one. Because these have been recorded within you, they follow you like your shadow and come out again later, with a different shape. But when they arise through your own consciousness, it's very easy to mistake those thoughts and feelings for "me."

Let's take a deeper look at these. Even though you make up your mind to do something good or to behave well, it often happens that you wind up doing the exact opposite, doesn't it? That happens because of the functioning of karmic consciousnesses—they prevent you from thinking and perceiving wisely.

Because you are the one who has input these karmic records, you are also the one who decides what to do when they come back out: will you erase them or will you re-create them?

The first step is not to blame others for what you experience, or to wish hardships or trouble upon them. Next, when these consciousnesses arise, let go of them and entrust what you're experiencing to your foundation. This is the way to dissolve these karmic records, instead of allowing them to multiply.

Think about what kind of thoughts you are giving rise to. If, while alive, you often give rise to thoughts that are like those of an animal or a demon, then after death that is the level existence you will feel the most affinity towards, and that is the level you will be drawn towards. Thus, it will be hard to avoid being reborn at that level.

On the other hand, if you cultivate sincere and kind thoughts, you'll be naturally drawn toward heavenly realms.

2. Dog Meat and the Seon Master

Long ago a renowned seon master settled in the deep mountains with several disciples.

As news of his presence spread through the region, many hundreds of sunims began to gather, wanting to practice under such a famous master.

One day, in front of the assembled monks, he called out in a powerful voice: "Everyone's looking rundown and tired. Go and catch several dogs and make dog soup for everyone."

The sunims sat in shocked silence. After the seon master left, the assembly erupted.

"What's he talking about? Sunims killing and eating a dog?"

"What kind of monk can't keep even the five basic precepts? Who would call him a teacher?"

"He's nothing like his reputation!"

They complained on and on, and soon began leaving in small groups.

After a while, only the original sunims and a few newcomers were left. The seon master looked around at everyone and chuckled, "The leaves that drop with the first breeze are gone now."

"In truth, there's no fundamental difference between Buddhas and unenlightened beings. It's just that people have such huge differences in their spiritual development and their ability to understand.

So sometimes a sieve has to be used to find those who are ready.

"Now, let's look at how to practice…."

✸

Good, bad, high, low, attractive, repulsive—these are all discriminations that originate from our fixed ideas.

When seen from the perspective of our foundation, everything is one interconnected whole. Every thing and life in the universe is connected to each of us through this foundation.

Remind yourself that every single thing originates from your foundation; entrust it with everything that confronts you and move forward. If you do this, all fixed ideas will naturally fade away, along with the habit of making discriminations. Then, you won't be misled by views, such as seeing some sunim as either a great practitioner or a fraud. You won't be caught by fixed ideas such as eating meat or not eating meat, nor will you criticize other people, claiming that they are hindering your practice.

If you want to awaken to the great meaning, never forget the fact that your inherent Buddha-nature is luminous, pure, and endowed with the infinite energy of the universe. Rely upon this Buddha-nature of yours in all things, and never let yourself be shaken, neither by events of the world around you, nor by thoughts and emotions arising from within.

Look at a great tree; it isn't shaken when some leaves fall away, nor does it tremble if a branch is broken. Although there are people in every generation who say that the Buddha-dharma is about to die out, you should know this: because mind exists, life will come into creation.

And wherever there is life, even if it is only a single being, the Buddha-dharma will be alive and vibrant.

3. A Greedy Daughter-in-law

Deep in the mountains of Korea, there lived a young man and his elderly mother. They were very poor, and the son was always working at some job or another in order to take care of his mother.

One day, as the village elders were sitting around chatting, the conversation turned to the young man. They all admired how hard he worked to take care of his mother, and as they talked, they realized that the young man had no other family to arrange a marriage for him. Then and there, the village elders decided that they would find him a wife.

They searched throughout the district, looking for a woman of good character willing to marry a poor farmer. At last they found a woman who seemed like a good match for the young man. She appeared gentle and caring, and like him was from a poor family. The elders made the arrangements, and the two of them were soon married.

Not long after the wedding, the young man began to realize that his new wife wasn't quite as kind and selfless as everyone had thought.

She was never satisfied with the money he earned, and to make matters worse, when he was out working in the fields, she treated his mother harshly and often wouldn't prepare proper meals for her. With each passing week, his mother was getting thinner and weaker.

As the young man thought about his wife's behavior and struggled with his anger, he tried to think about the situation from his wife's perspective.

"Well, it can't be easy being the wife of a poor farmer, trying to make do when there's never enough. At the temple they say that our basic nature is inherently good and compassionate, so if I treat her with compassion and caring, maybe I can draw forth those things from within her. Then, perhaps she'll behave better towards my mother."

He tried this approach, but instead of getting better, his wife's behavior only seemed to worsen. Finally, he realized that he couldn't wait for his wife to change her behavior; he would have to do something himself. He reflected deeply upon the situation for several days, until at last an idea occurred to him.

The end of the harvest season was approaching, and with it his yearly trip to the district capital to sell their grain. Normally, it took him over two weeks to make the round trip, but this time he hurried home, arriving a week earlier than expected.

He rushed into their courtyard, shouting for his wife. When she came out, he looked around to see if anyone else was listening and lowered his voice:

"You won't believe what I saw in the city! I stumbled into a side alley off the big market, and found a street where people were buying and selling grandmothers! The plump ones were going for a thousand strings of copper coins! Let's sell my mother there! A thousand strings of coins, as easy as snapping your fingers!

"Do you think we could get that much for her? She's kind of scrawny...."

"Hmm. You're right. We'll have to fatten her up first. But not a word to anyone. If other people start selling their mothers, we won't get a good price."

A thousand strings of coins was a huge amount of money, and the wife wanted it all. Late into the night all she could think about were ways to make her mother-in-law plump and healthy-looking. As the days went by, she experimented with different foods and medicines reputed to be good for the elderly. Eventually, she became obsessed with her mother-in-law's health.

With this kind of care, her mother-in-law began to recover. One day, as she took her grandson for a walk, she met some old friends and spoke with amazement about how well her daughter-in-law was taking care of her.

Over the next months, stories about how well the wife looked after her mother-in-law spread throughout the surrounding villages, and even reached the ears of the district governor.

Impressed, he ordered a stone monument to be erected, commemorating her behavior and holding it forth as a model of virtue for others.

The wife had started with the intention of getting rich, but as she spent day after day thinking about someone other than herself, her own greed and selfishness had begun to melt away. Seeing the stone monument was the final straw; she broke down into tears, determined to truly become the person described there.

※

Our fundamental mind, our Buddha-nature, contains infinite wisdom. However, this isn't something you can find without making an effort.

Like the young man, you have to diligently reflect inwardly and return your questions inwardly, while searching for a solution that will benefit everyone. If you do this, then the wisdom of your Buddha-nature can come forth.

No matter how great the wisdom, you won't see any results from it without ceaseless effort and strong faith. If you want to achieve something in your life, throw away self-centeredness and greed, and then, with faith, entrust everything to your foundation.

While continuing to observe and being patient, use both your body and mind to put your understanding into practice. If you can make this kind of effort, you will certainly find the best way forward.

4. Red Bean Porridge

Long ago there was a famous abbess whose style of teaching was quite different from other Buddhist masters.

She didn't teach sutras, nor did she emphasize the many precepts that monastics must uphold. She left the affairs of daily life up to the sunims themselves, and when she entrusted a nun with a particular job or assignment, she gave her complete authority to take care of things however she saw fit. In fact, there was only one thing she continually emphasized:

"Spiritual practice and daily life don't exist apart from each other. Everything that arises throughout our daily life is what we've previously made. It's been recorded within our foundation and returns to us one by one with a different shape. Every single thing arises from our foundation, so it is to there that we have to return everything that confronts us.

"This is true regardless of whether something arises from inside or seems to come from outside of ourselves. You have to return every single thing to your foundation without the least attachment, and let them melt down there.

"Do this, and the difficulties and hardships you face will melt down and come back out as positive things."

When new sunims first heard of entrusting everything to one's foundation, they tended to think it was fairly simple and easy to practice.

The nun who was in charge of the cooking also had a similar thought.

"Ah! Of course, everything arises from our foundation, so that's where I need to return everything. Hah! What could be simpler?!"

However, actually doing this in the middle of her life proved to be more than a little difficult. Not only were there a large number of sunims, which meant a large quantity of food to prepare, but the food could never be late. All of the dishes had to be ready when the meal bell rang and the sunims gathered.

So, the nun in charge of the kitchen was always tired, and often exhausted. Moreover, on days with special ceremonies or memorials, there was so much work that anyone would need two bodies to keep up with it all.

The cook was forever trying to take care of all the urgent tasks that kept arising, and it often seemed that for every one she resolved, two more came to take its place. Entrusting everything to her inherent foundation was turning out to be harder than the kitchen nun had expected.

On top of everything else, she was cooking for a large group, so no matter how much thought or care she put into the meals, someone was always complaining. They didn't like the flavor, or it had no flavor, or it was too salty, or it was too spicy, and so on.

At first she was just hurt, but with time and fatigue, she found herself getting more and more resentful.

"What on earth am I working so hard for? Not one of them seems to appreciate what I'm doing. I'm up every morning before sunrise, preparing their meals—would it kill them to offer a word of thanks?"

As the months went by, feelings of being mistreated boiled up within her, and she began to realize how often she was getting caught up in these thoughts. She remembered what the abbess had said about returning everything to her inherent foundation, so she redoubled her efforts to actually let go and entrust all the things that were confronting her.

Some time later, the kitchen nun was preparing the traditional red-bean porridge that was served every year on the winter solstice. There was a lot of extra work that day, and she began to fall back into the thought that no one appreciated the work she did. Distracted by this, she built too big of a fire.

The pot she used for the porridge was a huge one, cast iron and over a meter in diameter. By the time she realized that she'd used too much wood, the porridge had already reached the boiling point. Large bubbles began to rise to the surface and burst, splattering the nun with boiling hot porridge and driving her away from the pot.

She stood back a safe distance and just watched the bubbles as they continuously arose in the porridge. Suddenly she felt like she'd been hit by lightning:

"Ho! Those bubbles aren't coming from somewhere else! Every single one is arising from inside of the pot, and I made it happen! All of the resentment and anger I've been feeling has arisen from how I used my mind!

"I'm the one who has made those things, and yet I kept blaming others. How could I have been so ignorant? Without a doubt, this agitation has been my foundation working to clear up my ignorance!"

At last, she truly understood what the abbess had meant. She stood in front of that pot of porridge, and as each bubble arose in the thick liquid, she would exclaim, "This one's the Bodhisattva of Wisdom! That one's the Bodhisattva of Compassion! Hey, over there is the Buddha!"

As the bubbles swelled up, she gently popped them, and watched as they collapsed in on themselves. After a while, when the red-bean porridge had cooked for just the right amount of time, no more bubbles arose, and they no longer threatened to splatter people near the kettle.

The porridge had reached the point where it could feed everyone.

Like the kitchen nun, who saw all of those messy bubbles as Bodhisattvas and Buddhas and knew that they were not separate from her foundation, we, too, have to remember that regardless of the form things take, they all arise from our foundation.

So that's where we have to return them. And this doesn't just apply to the things that arise within our minds—it's also the things that occur in front of us in our daily lives. These are also what we've made, what we've input into our foundation, and which have merely returned to us with a different form.

Absolutely everything, without exception, has to be returned to our foundation. It's all something we've created, but we also have the power to change it, so are we going to just keep staring at it?

If we keep letting go, then like the porridge, our minds will ripen. In the richness of a fully ripened mind, you will come to understand for yourself the profound functioning of the Dharma, and taste life as it should be.

5. Making a Mirror

The great Chan Master Nanyue[3] was the abbot of Prajna Temple, when a young, unknown monk named Mazu[4] arrived.

Mazu worked hard, studying with the other monks and spending hour after hour sitting in the meditation hall. Carefully observing him, Master Nanyue perceived that he was close to breaking through the web of illusion and so perceiving his true Buddha essence.

Thus, one afternoon Master Nanyue sat down beside Mazu and started polishing a roof tile. Mazu had no idea why his teacher was doing this, but he kept his curiosity to himself and didn't say anything. This continued for several days until at last Mazu couldn't contain himself.

"Master, why on earth are you polishing a tile?"

"I'm trying to turn it into a mirror." In those days mirrors were made from pieces of metal polished to a high shine.

---

3. **Nanyue Huairang** (南嶽懷讓, 677~744): Considered one of the greatest disciples of the Sixth Patriarch, Huineng.
4. **Mazu Daoyi** (馬祖道一, 709~788): One of the greatest chan masters of China. Students in his lineage would go on to found the majority of the chan lineages in China and Korea.

"How can polishing possibly make a piece of tile into a mirror? No matter how much you polish it, clay can't shine forth."

"And how can crossing your legs and sitting down make you a Buddha?" responded Nanyue.

Mazu felt like he'd suddenly been hit with a log! Almost forgetting to breathe, he asked Nanyue, "Then what should I do?"

"Let me ask you one thing. If an ox cart won't move, do you hit the cart or do you hit the ox?"

At that instant, Mazu became deeply enlightened.

It's the ox that moves the cart. In this story, the ox represents our mind, and the cart is our body. Ultimately, these two can't be split apart.

However, some people focus exclusively on mind and ignore the body, while others put the body through all kinds of training and neglect mind.

If mind is upright, then one's body and behavior also become upright. And if you're keeping your body and behavior upright, the strength to keep your mind upright also arises. So you can't say that one is more important than the other. Further, without a body, you can't engage in spiritual practice. Both are necessary.

Nonetheless, mind is the center. Mind is the foundation of everything, the root. When growing a tree, if you pay attention to only the branches and leaves and ignore the roots, how could that tree flourish? Similarly, mind, not the body, needs to be the ultimate focus of spiritual practice in order to awaken.

Your fundamental mind also needs to be the focus of your daily life. You probably already know this, but there are times when you misbehave and speak unwisely, aren't there? These things happen because you aren't entrusting everything to your foundation, due to the influence of your habits and karmic consciousnesses. If you're just acting based upon your intellect and limited perceptions, how could you not fall into unwise speech and actions?

We are each endowed with this essence that transcends time and space, and connects us all. It has existed since even before we were born, so entrust it with everything. Each one of us must explore and investigate this fundamental mind and then apply and experiment with what we learn.

Trust in the ability of your fundamental mind and live your daily life with wisdom and confidence.

6. Parents' Endless Love

Long ago there was a couple who seemed destined to remain childless. Finally, after many years of prayer, they had a son.

He was the center of their world, the child they had longed for, and they raised him with great love and devotion. But their care didn't seem to affect his character at all, and he grew up to be selfish and greedy.

Soon after he married, he and his wife secretly sold his parents' fields and cattle, and then ran away with the money. His parents had their small house and that was it; everything else was gone. Can you imagine how angry and betrayed they must have felt?

Although hurting terribly, they still loved their son very much and expected that sooner or later he would return. As time went by with no sign of him or his wife, they began to worry.

"Our land and cattle wouldn't have brought that much money. What will happen to them once they've gone through it?"

Every day they prayed for them, that wherever they were, their lives would be free of hardships and hunger, disasters and illness.

The parents continued to live in the same house for as long as they could, hoping that someday their son would return. But as their savings ran out, they had to sell their house; eventually this money was exhausted as well, and they had no place to go.

Fortunately, a large temple in the area was familiar with their situation and arranged for the elderly couple to come and live there. The wife worked in the kitchens, helping to prepare meals, while her husband helped collect firewood and tend the fires.

A few years later the husband passed away, and his wife followed him soon after. The husband was reborn in a nearby village, and a few years later his wife was reborn as his neighbor. Eventually, they both ended up becoming monks at that very temple.

One day, the younger of the two monks was traveling on an important errand. Passing a dilapidated hut beside the road, he happened to look inside, where he saw a very poor, elderly couple huddled together. They looked ill and were so skinny that if he had tried, he probably could have counted all their bones.

The wife didn't even have any clothes; instead, she wore an old rice sack with holes cut out for her head and arms. Her husband was wearing pants and a shirt, or what must have once been pants and a shirt; now they looked more like rags strung together. They would take turns wearing this one set of clothes, and the one with the clothes would go out begging for food.

The younger monk had to hurry on his way, but as he thought about them, he realized that they would probably die within a week or two if nothing were done to help. Upon returning to the temple, he went to see his older Dharma brother and told him about what he'd seen.

About this time, their teacher entered the room. After hearing the whole story, he chuckled, and then sighed. "There's no escaping from karma. In your last life, you two were a married couple, and those old people were your children. One was your son and the other your daughter-in-law."

Hearing the entire story, the monks were shocked and heartbroken. The elder monk wondered out loud, "If we spent so much effort praying for their well-being, how could such a fate have befallen them?"

Their teacher answered with a sad voice. "I understand how much you wanted to help them, but people receive things in proportion to what they have done. You two have received the fruits of what you did, and they've received the fruits of what they did. Although you wanted to lead them to a better way of living, their hearts were so full of greed, anger, and foolishness that there was no room left to receive your prayers and compassion."

By now, tears were streaming down the faces of both monks. "Isn't there anything we can do to help them?"

Their teacher was silent for several minutes, then asked, "Were they too sick to go out and help others?"

The younger monk nodded.

"Well, they need to do something for someone else. All their lives they've thought of only themselves, and without the virtue that comes from generosity, it will be hard to make a connection with them and lead them forward. Didn't they have anything?"

"No," answered the younger monk, "just the clothes on their back and a rice sack for a blanket."

"Well, that will have to do. Go back and have them donate their clothes. It's everything they own, so in that sense, it's a huge donation. With your help, that might be enough to break through the damage created by their greed and desire."

"But, their clothes...," sobbed the younger monk.

"I know," sighed their teacher, tears welling up in his eyes.

So, the younger monk went back to the old couple, and trying not to cry, told them to donate their one set of filthy, threadbare clothes. He couldn't bring himself to repeat what he'd heard from his teacher, but as the old couple complained bitterly, the monk finally yelled at them, "Donate your clothes! It's the only thing that can help you!"

The old man took the clothes off and threw them in a stinking pile at the monk's feet. Later, the old couple cut the rice sack in half, each one using their half like a shawl; but a whole or half a sack made little difference, and in their near naked state they were too ashamed to even beg for food.

The younger monk carried the clothes back to the temple on the end of a stick. Both he and his brother monk deeply reflected on how they could make this offering as worthy as possible. So, after washing and boiling the clothes, they used what was left of the shirt to clean the Dharma hall, and with the pants they cleaned the monks' rooms.

They did this every morning and evening until the rags were useless even for cleaning. Finally, they burned the rags and mixed the ashes with water, which they both drank up.

How can I express their sincerity? In the past as parents, and in this life as monks, their caring and love was that deep.

After some days had passed, the local villagers began to wonder what had happened to the two old beggars. "Well, they haven't been around for a while, so they've probably died, haven't they? Still, I suppose we should go and check."

With this, a group of men and women went to the hut, and what they found moved them all. The old couple lay together, sick and shaking with fever. Left alone, they would certainly die before long. The villagers discussed the situation for a few minutes, and everyone was in agreement: they would bring the old couple back with them, and the whole village would look after them.

Over the next few months, each family took turns feeding and caring for the old couple. Receiving so much kindness, old couple began to think about how they had treated their own parents. They went to the temple and asked to speak with the monk who had come to their hut a few months before.

The two monks and their teacher greeted the old couple and listened intently to what they said.

"We've done some terrible things, and the suffering that resulted was like a living death. But then you came by and everything changed. We only did what you told us, to donate our clothes, but the merit of that alone has caused us to live comfortably these last few months.

"But what about our parents? We did such a terrible thing to them. What happened to them after we left? We left them with nothing. How could we have treated our parents like that?" By now, the old couple was crying hard as they spoke.

"Your mother and father are right in front of you—they are these two monks!" said the teacher.

The old couple couldn't believe their ears. The teacher continued, "The previous shape and appearance of your parents has disappeared; now they stand before you as these two monks. As your parents, their love and prayers for you were complete and unconditional.

"Likewise, in this life also, they received your donation with complete sincerity and used that old shirt to clean the Dharma hall, and the pants to clean the monks' quarters. And when those rags were nothing but threads, they burned them and drank the ashes. This is how deep and unconditional a parent's love is."

Hearing this, the old couple collapsed. The monks revived them, but the old couple couldn't say a word. They sobbed for breath as tears washed their faces. In an instant, they had seen all of the suffering they had caused their parents, as well as all the blessings they'd thrown away.

Their regret at how they'd lived and the desire to follow a wiser path seemed to burst their hearts. Bathed in love and compassion, they died there, in the arms of the monks who had been their parents.

The couple's parents had embraced them with love instead of curses, viewing everything their children had done as part of their own karma. Instead of getting angry or depressed over it, they worked at returning it to their foundation.

Thus, they were able to respond wisely, in a way that eventually led their children to see an alternative to the way they had been living. As the parents entrusted everything back to their true nature, they and their children became one, and the light that arose from this helped free their children from their ignorance and misguided views.

By freeing their children like this, the parents also saved themselves.

※

Although you do something for someone else, ultimately you're the one who will benefit. And if you do something harmful, that doesn't just fade away. Eventually it will all return to you.

If you understand only these two truths, how could you just drift through life? Be diligent; do your very best with the things that arise in your life. Be utterly sincere in the things you do. Then the things you do for yourself end up benefiting others as well, and the things you do for others will also benefit you.

If you only think about yourself and your own difficulties, while ignoring the situation of those around you, how could this be called the correct path? Once we are born into this world, it's as if we are all riding in the same boat.

Even if you only have a little to eat, share it with those who have less. If everyone practices like this, there will be more than enough for everyone.

7. The Man Who Ran Out of Merit

Long ago there was a poor man who did his best to live an honest life. Although prosperity was a stranger to his home, he worked hard to avoid getting caught up in desire or envy. He never cheated others, and instead tried to be satisfied with what little he did have.

It seemed to him that he was living a good life, and he assumed that after his death he would find himself in a good place.

On the day he died, he arrived in the next world, but instead of the heavenly realm he expected, he saw a vast darkness lit only by a huge assembly of candles.

There were thin candles and great thick candles, candles so tall he could barely see their tops and little stubby candles. There were candles that burned with a bright flame, and candles that always seemed on the verge of going out. In front of each candle was a pouch with a person's name on it; some of these pouches looked like they were stuffed full, and others were limp and empty.

Looking around, he saw that one of the empty pouches had his own name on it, and the candle behind it, though only half burned, had gone out.

As he moved closer to the empty pouch, an old man appeared and began speaking:

"I am the guardian of this place, and I am also your ancestor, although by your reckoning that was nine generations ago. The candles you see represent the amount of life a person is born with, and the pouches represent the merit and virtue they have.

"This merit and virtue arises from their selfless thoughts and actions, and sometimes it's inherited from their ancestors. Your ancestors also accumulated a great deal of virtue and merit, but it was all gone by your generation. People just kept taking and taking, without putting anything back.

"You could have lived longer, but died young because you ran out of merit. Although you lived a good life without causing harm to others, you didn't do much for them, either. You didn't accumulate any extra merit and virtue, nor was any left of what your ancestors created. However, you led an honest life, and that's not an easy thing when one is so poor.

"Nine generations ago, I did much to relieve the suffering of others, and much to help brighten their minds. Because of this I became the guardian of this place, and because of our connection you were able to come here. So, there may be a way I can help you." The old man pointed to a very tall candle nearby, and explained:

"This man still has many, many more years of life left. He also has quite a bit of merit and good fortune stored up, but eight years must pass before he is allowed to use it. So, I'll lend you his merit and good fortune until then.

"Go back to the living world and help many others while leading a good life. Then, when the time comes, there will be enough accumulated merit to pay him back, with plenty left over for you. You seem to be someone who would use his blessings to help others, so let's give this a try. Remember, in eight years all debts will have to be settled."

With this last reminder, the old man sent him back to this world.

Back at his home, people had gathered for the poor man's funeral and were paying their last respects when his spirit suddenly returned to his body. It was probably due to his newly borrowed merit that his return wasn't the cause of an additional funeral or two!

The poor man never forgot what his ancestor had told him, and for eight years he worked in all kinds of ways to relieve people's suffering and help them live brighter lives. In this way, the merit and virtue of his actions paid back that which he had borrowed. Meanwhile, every business venture he undertook was hugely successful, to the point where eventually he became one of the richest men in the province.

Finally, one day there appeared at his gate a very poor, bedraggled man. In return for food and a dry place to sleep, he offered to work as a servant, saying that he was willing to do all of the hardest and dirtiest jobs.

As soon as the rich man saw his face, he knew this was the person whose merit and fortune he had borrowed, and that the time to finish paying off all debts had arrived. He invited the poor man into his home and proceeded to give him the house and half of everything else he owned.

Having repaid his debt, the man continued to prosper and do good works up until the very end. The example he set inspired his children and grandchildren, and for generation after generation his descendants were a bright light of wisdom and compassion to all around them.

※

If you're curious about your past, look at how you're living right now. It's the same if you want to know about your future: look at how you're living right now.

Hardships occur in exact proportion to the debts we've incurred. If we act without realizing what we're doing, then when the results of those actions and thoughts return to us, we won't understand why we're experiencing those things.

On the other hand, if we understand what we are doing as we do it, then we'll understand when the results of those actions return to us. Look at how you are living now, and you can know what your future will be.

Everybody knows how to save money for the future, so why don't people think more about these invisible savings that will affect us life after life?

8. The General's Strange Dream

One night, the general in charge of Korea's northern armies, Sung-gye Yi, was having a very strange dream.

Crows were cawing loudly above the palace, as a large glass mirror shattered into a thousand pieces at his feet. Meanwhile, outside his window, flowers bloomed but then immediately withered away, and high on his gate, hanging by its neck, a scarecrow was swinging in the wind.

Sung-gye Yi awoke with an ominous feeling. His dream was so dark and weird that it bothered him for many days. He was one of the Goryeo Dynasty's top generals, and he had fought in countless battles both large and small. He always fought at the front of his army, and was known for his fearlessness. He'd faced death time after time and seen many gruesome things, yet this dream, with its strange omens, gnawed at him.

Finally, he decided to go and ask his teacher about it. This was a pretty good idea, because his teacher was the great Buddhist monk Muhak, who was wise beyond imagining. The general humbly explained his dream to Muhak and asked what he should do.

The great monk was silent, and for several long moments the general felt as if Muhak were staring into his very soul. At last, Muhak slowly smiled. "The dream means you're going to be king."

He began to explain the meaning of the omens: "Crows always caw when someone new comes into the area, and in your dream they're cawing because a new master is coming to the royal palace. The sound of the breaking mirror is the voices of a great multitude asking you to be their leader. The withered flowers mean that your diligence is about to bear fruit, while the dangling scarecrow high over the gate means that you will be someone everybody looks up to."

As he listened, General Yi was both relieved and surprised by what Muhak told him.

Just as the great monk predicted, he went on to become the first king of the Joseon Dynasty, which lasted for over five hundred years.

The great master Muhak didn't interpret the dream based upon rigid ideas of some signs being good and others being bad.

He just returned everything to his foundation and relayed the thoughts that arose from there. Even if you see terrifying ghosts or disasters in your dreams, don't be disturbed by those images. Instead, just return them to your foundation and raise good thoughts.

Don't be deceived—everything is the manifestation of your foundation, what is called *Juingong*.[5] Juingong means the true doer, which is without any fixed shape. Everyone is endowed with this, and it is the foundation through which we are connected to everything else.

It is the beginning and end of everything, but it is always changing and manifesting, without a fixed form or shape. So take even the things that arise in a dream and return them to your foundation.

If you practice like this in both your dreams and your waking life, you'll live with confidence and equanimity, undaunted by good or bad events.

---

5. **Juingong** [ju-in-gong] (主人空): "Juin(主人)" means the true doer or the master, and "gong(空)" means empty. Thus Juingong is our true nature, our true essence, the master within that is always changing and manifesting, without a fixed form or shape.

9. The Fox that Fell in a Hole

Once there was a fox who was being chased by a tiger. He ran this way and that, but the tiger was always right behind him. Glancing over his shoulder, the fox suddenly stumbled into a deep, narrow hole.

The tiger reached down, trying to catch the fox with his claws, but the hole was too deep. He paced back and forth around the hole, but finaly returned to the forest.

Now, try as the fox might, he couldn't climb out of that hole. He jumped and he scratched, but each time he slid back down. Stuck there with no food and only dew for water, fear began to fill him: What if he could never escape?

However, as one day and then another went by, something strange occurred: the fox's thoughts began to settle down, and eventually he entered a state of deep contemplation. Suddenly, for just an instant, the fox's true nature shone through.

Indra, who rules the heavenly realms, knew at that moment what had happened. He came down to the forest and bowed deeply to the fox, saying, "Even though you have the body of a fox, you have achieved the stage of seeing your own nature. How wonderful!"

The fox had no idea what Indra was talking about; he just wanted to get out of that hole. In a strangled voice, he cried out, "What good is bowing?! If you want to help, get me out of here!"

Indra smiled and freed the fox in an instant. Then, he did something very strange: he gave the fox a beautiful set of embroidered silk clothes.

Again, the fox stared at Indra in amazement. "Look at my body! What possible use could I have for clothes?!"

With this, the fox turned and leapt back into the forest, without even a word of thanks.

※

You may have realized that the fox represents human beings, the tiger is truth, and Indra is enlightenment.

The fox was chased by the tiger into a place from which there was no escape, until at last, after confronting many difficult things, the fox perceived his inherent nature. Whether we know it or not, we, too, are in the same situation.

In giving the fox such beautiful clothes, Indra was trying to show the fox his inherent potential and encourage him to become a much higher being.

Unfortunately, the fox didn't understand this, because although he had been freed from one hole, he was still not free from the pit of his own habits and fixed ideas.

If the fox had been able to throw away his habits and views centered on his physical body, he would have realized that he, the tiger, and Indra were all one. Then the fox would have been able to put on the silk clothing without being blocked by his preconceived ideas.

No matter how many sutras you've read, or how much hard training you've undergone, no matter that you may have even glimpsed your inherent nature, unless you apply yourself further and deeply awaken, it will be hard to avoid becoming a fox who is still trapped by his own habits and fixed ways of thinking.

10. The Man who Became a Cow

On a remote farm in the mountains of Gangwon Province, there lived an old man, together with his son and daughter-in-law and their many children.

The old man had worked hard at spiritual cultivation for many decades, and he took everything that arose in life as something to be used for spiritual practice. So, although he was quite poor, he never felt a sense of lack, and his bright laughter and wisdom spread to everyone around him. All in all, theirs was a happy family.

Sadly, one day his son suddenly died. Not long after this, the old man began to sense that he, too, didn't have much time left. The old man's greatest concern was his daughter-in-law. He knew all too well how hard it would be for her to work the farm by herself while raising five young children.

After much meditation, he knew what he would do: he would be reborn as a cow in order to help his family.

Thus, several months after his death, the family's elderly cow gave birth to a strong, bright-eyed calf. As the calf grew, it seemed to know what work needed to be done on the farm even before the woman.

For example, when it was time to plow the fields, the cow would stand next to the plow and moo loudly until the daughter-in-law understood.

The cow helped the woman in many other ways, too. One day while working in the fields, she was bitten by a snake. Her ankle swelled up and became infected, and within a few days she couldn't move; she could only lie in her room, moaning from the pain.

Her children were too young to help her, but the cow came up to the house and kept hitting its tail on the porch. Finally, she crawled out to see what was going on.

The cow nudged her up on its back and carried her to a spring far in the mountains. It stunk of rotten eggs, but the cow gently set her down so that her leg lay soaking in the spring. Within a few hours, the swelling began to go down and her fever broke. Without the cow's help, it's likely she would have died.

In this way, twenty years flew by. One by one, all of her children grew up and left home, until only she and the cow were left. One evening, she fell asleep early and had a strange dream.

Her father-in-law, whom she hadn't thought of in years, appeared and spoke to her:

"I knew how difficult your life was going to be, trying to raise children and run a farm by yourself. So, to help ease your way, I was reborn as your cow.

"I'm leaving now, but another aspect of myself is living in a small hermitage on the other side of this mountain range. If you would like to practice together, go to that temple."

The daughter-in-law awoke with a start and ran barefoot out to the cow, but it had already died. She knelt there and cried, awed by the love of her father-in-law, who was willing to be reborn as even a cow in order to help her.

When the sun came up, she left for the temple her father-in-law had told her about in the dream. After traveling for several days, she found the hermitage, and saw that a young sunim was living there alone. He was about twenty years old, and looked exactly like her father-in-law—his face even had a mole in the same place.

Amazingly, her father-in-law had been reborn as both the cow and the sunim.

※

The ability and functioning of mind is so profound that most people can't begin to imagine it.

Look at a single cup of water—it can't do much, can it? However, if you add that cup of water to the ocean, then its combined strength becomes unimaginable.

This is the strength of our fundamental Buddha-essence.

But how can we know this when we spend each day lost in a thousand different kinds of discriminations? When we just stop chasing these, and instead return them all to our fundamental nature, then the energy of our fundamental mind and the energy of everything we encounter will be able to function together as one.

The energy of this combined functioning is beyond anything you can imagine. It dwarfs even that of the oceans and skies, for it is the energy of every single thing in the universe, connected and working as one.

If you truly want to help someone, let go of all your discriminations. Let go unconditionally of all of your ideas about high and low, worthy and unworthy, human or animal.

When you keep entrusting everything to your fundamental essence in this way, something deep within you will stir. This vast energy responds to whatever is needed and takes any form. It leaves no trace of its passage, yet it's more powerful than the heavens and earth.

It is true compassion, and can take any shape—even that of a cow.

11. Ananda and the Keyhole

Not long after the Buddha entered Nirvana, a council of his disciples was called. Five hundred of the Buddha's greatest disciples gathered together and chose Kassapa to head the council. Their purpose was to collect all of the different teachings of the Buddha.

Much to everyone's surprise, Kassapa refused to allow the Buddha's attendant Ananda to join them. Kassapa explained:

"The Buddha taught us that everything in this world is the non-dual functioning and interaction of the material realm and the nonmaterial realm. Thus, we must be able to take care of things while combining both realms, without neglecting either side.

"However, because Ananda is still stuck in the mind of discriminations, he has not combined with his foundation and so is unable to harmoniously use both sides.

"Thus, even though he perfectly remembers every word of the Buddha, without knowing this foundation, how can he understand the true meaning of what the Buddha said? How then could he correctly transmit the Buddha's intention? I cannot allow him to attend."

Among the ten great disciples of the Buddha, it was Ananda who had heard the most talks by the Buddha, and it was Ananda whose memory was nearly perfect. So you can imagine how shocked and embarrassed he was at being excluded from the council.

Kassapa's words were hard to hear and hard to accept for Ananda, but he knew that Kassapa's enlightenment and practice were acknowledged by all of the great disciples, even by the Buddha himself.

Thus, Ananda made up his mind to awaken. He stayed in his room without eating or sleeping, never allowing his attention to be diverted outwardly. Instead, he focused all of his attention inward, forgetting about even life and death.

He took every single thing that arose and entrusted it to his inherent nature, the true doer. He let go of every kind of thought of "me" and "you," "I" and "mine." As he entrusted everything, his only desire was to become one with his true self.

One night, everything became clear. In a great moment he realized what Kassapa had meant when he described combining with the foundation and harmoniously using both sides. Ananda was so happy that he ran all the way to where the council was gathered and started banging on the outer gate.

From inside, Kassapa asked, "Who's there?"

"It's me, Ananda!"

"What do you want at this time of night?"

"Oh, Kassapa!! I've done it! I've done it! Now I understand why I couldn't be allowed to attend the council!" shouted Ananda.

Kassapa was delighted to hear that at last Ananda, too, had awakened. "Well done! If you want to join us, just come in through the keyhole."

As soon as Ananda heard Kassapa, he rushed in through the keyhole and bowed to the assembly. Then the two disciples hugged each other and cried for joy.

∗∗∗

This is the story of how Ananda came to join the council, but you must see more than the words alone.

When you awaken to your true nature, you will be able to see and hear everything through your mind's eye. You'll realize that every single thing is inherently connected and functions as one. As soon as Ananda had awakened, he could perceive Kassapa's mind, and he knew that Kassapa was not separate from himself.

Ananda entering through the keyhole means that Ananda's mind went back and forth freely, because from the very beginning all beings are connected as one through our fundamental mind.

The Buddha once said, "It's hard to find the door because there are so many doors. And it's hard to find the door because there is no door." Everything in this world is an entryway, an open door to the Buddha-dharma, so what need is there to worry about locks or keyholes?

You need to take a close look at yourself. You will not understand the Buddha-dharma, which is the non-dual functioning of the entire world, by frantically trying to find some separate, unique method or key.

Be careful that you're not trying to understand the Buddha's teachings through only theory and intellect. Question yourself carefully! Check whether you truly understand the deep meaning, or instead have only a vague and superficial understanding.

Things don't follow fixed paths, so don't get caught up in fixed ideas that things will happen in certain ways. Just keep entrusting everything to your foundation, and the truth of the world will naturally become clear.

Once the water calms down, the moon shines forth.

An ancient pine tree
sends forth
a bolt of lightning,
and rain falls across the world.
As the deep oceans fill,
fish
both big and small
begin to sing and dance.

Seon Master Daehaeng
November 19, 1989

12. Worm Soup

The teacher at a small, remote temple was quite ill, and gradually became weaker and weaker. The sunims who practiced there began to worry because they had nothing in the way of medicine to give him.

One day, the most junior sunim suddenly remembered something he had heard years before: for an illness that involved severe weakness, a broth made from fresh earthworms would help someone recover their strength. He rushed to tell his Dharma brothers, but upon hearing this, they sharply criticized him for even thinking about violating the precept of not killing.

Although the junior sunim didn't want to hurt any living creatures, his teacher's condition was rapidly getting worse.

"If earthworm soup can help our teacher recover, then I'll make it, even if I have to spend some time in hell," he decided.

He must have collected nearly a hundred earthworms, which he cleaned and boiled in a huge pot. As he made the broth, he was thinking about the worms:

"I'm sorry for treating you like this, but you may be able to help our teacher recover."

To repay the worms, he entrusted the following thoughts to his inherent nature:

"Your mind and my mind are one mind. Experiencing this oneness, may you be reborn at the highest level you're comfortable with. Thank you all so much!"

Having made the earthworm soup in this way, every morning and every evening the sunim fed a bowl of the broth to his teacher.

The other sunims, however, couldn't believe what he'd done, and hounded him. "Have you forgotten the precept of not killing? Do you have any idea of the karma that will result from your actions?"

But the sunim was undisturbed. "Brothers, if there is any kind of punishment, I'll be the one to bear it. Anyway, it seems this broth is actually helping to save both our teacher and the worms. As they enter our teacher's body, they become one with him and his bright mind, and so evolve.

"How many thousands of years would it take for these worms to meet an enlightened person and experience that level of consciousness?

"So this is helping all of these worms, while at the same time reviving our teacher. They are saving each other!"

By the time their teacher had finished drinking all of the broth, his health had improved and his recovery seemed certain. He called for the young sunim. "That broth was full of energy and helped me a lot. But something was unusual about it—what was it made of?"

"Oh, I found an ancient tree in the forest and took some of the young leaves and boiled them for a long time," answered the young sunim.

His teacher's eyes narrowed, and before his penetrating gaze the young sunim felt as if all his inner secrets were revealed.

And then his teacher smiled.

※

What do you think about how the precepts should be upheld? Are you struggling to uphold them while focusing on only the material aspect of existence?

We can truly understand what needs to be done only when we can understand the unseen realm— then we can correctly understand the material realm and will be able to uphold the precepts as they were intended.

To put it another way, don't treat the spiritual and the material as separate. Do your best to combine them together and use them as one. This is upholding the precepts correctly.

Because every life is as precious as our own life and body, we are taught to not kill. The pain and suffering others experience is what we also experience. If you understand this, you can't treat other forms of life harshly.

However, it can sometimes happen that your actions deprive others of life, even though that wasn't your intention to cause them harm. If that happens, wholeheartedly entrust the entire situation to your foundation, Juingong, such that you and their mind are not separate.

Know that "their mind and my mind are not two," and entrust this thought to your foundation. Then, because you've entrusted their mind without separating it from your mind, you destroy only the other being's body, not its mind. To a certain extent, it can even be said that you've helped remove their ignorance.

Even so, don't needlessly kill or eat anything you like. Not everything can be justified. Killing that comes from desire, cruelty, and greed creates a terrible burden.

13. Buckwheat Dumplings

A century or so ago, in a remote meditation hall, the sunims were preparing to sit long into the night.

It had been a normal meditation retreat in all regards, until one sunim suddenly gave a great laugh and looked around, smiling, "Why is everyone sitting here so stiffly? Does our Buddha-nature only exist within the butt prints of our meditation cushions?"

As the sunims sat there, they felt each word strike home. Later, after some discussion, they asked that sunim to become their teacher.

One day he gave the other sunims a large sack of buckwheat seed and told them to plant it all. In those days there wasn't much to eat in a temple like that, and what they had was rough and basic, so the sunims' mouths began to water as they thought of all the foods they could make from buckwheat.

"We could make fine noodles with a savory sauce, or we could roast the buckwheat and have it as porridge, or we could make steamed cakes, or we could ..." and so their conversation went as they planted the buckwheat.

After the planting was finished, a couple of sunims were still brimming with thoughts of their future meal, and during tea they asked their teacher, "Sunim, will it be noodles or steamed cake, or something else?"

"Oh, that," he answered disinterestedly, "I suppose we'll have to wait and see."

The buckwheat grew and flowered, and as the nights grew longer, the grains grew fatter.

One hungry sunim not so subtly hinted, "Steamed buckwheat cakes would taste wonderful, wouldn't they?" But all he got from his teacher was an indifferent shrug.

Finally, it was time to harvest the buckwheat, and at last their teacher revealed what the food was to be: buckwheat dumplings in soup! As the sunims ground the buckwheat into flour, one sunim asked their teacher, "We're really going to have soup and dumplings?"

But their teacher replied, "When you put your spoon in your mouth, then you'll know!"

As the time for the noon meal approached, all of the sunims gathered together in the main hall. They chanted their thanks for the meal, and all together started eating the soup and dumplings. As soon as they put their spoons in their mouths, their teacher gave a great roar.

"Stop! Don't swallow it and don't spit it out!"

The sunims froze at the sound of his voice and just sat there, mouths full of hot soup.

After a bit, their teacher asked, "Do you have any soup or dumplings left?"

"I've got a bit left," one sunim answered.

"Don't swallow it and don't spit it out!"

Another sunim spoke up, "It's gone! They just dissolved and disappeared."

"What do you think happened then?" asked the teacher.

"Well, I didn't notice it, but it seems like it just dissolved and went down bit by bit."

"That's it exactly! You weren't trying to eat, and yet that food is gone. Do you understand the principle that underlies this?"

※

Dumplings are not dumplings, swallowing is not swallowing, and spitting out is not spitting out.

Although things exist individually, nonetheless, they're all connected together and function as one, changing and manifesting with every instant.

This also describes emptiness, wisdom, and Buddha; what is there that can be added or taken away? How could there truly be something called a hindrance? Don't let yourself be entangled by ideas such as "achieving enlightenment" or "finding wisdom."

Understand this principle and practice diligently. Wouldn't it be wonderful to eat this soup without getting caught up in ideas of eating or not eating, doing or not doing? Wouldn't it be wonderful to naturally dissolve and swallow the lumps in the soup?

Work hard to understand what it means when I say that the entire universe can be put into a single bowl, and that one bowl can hold it all perfectly.

14. Wonhyo's Awakening

When Wonhyo and Uisang were young monks, they decided to go to China to find a great master under whom they could study.

Leaving Gyeongju, the capital of the Silla Kingdom, they headed to the southwest coast of Korea to find a boat that could take them across the sea to China

After weeks of walking, they were nearing the coast. The sky had turned dark and the showers were fast becoming torrents. Before long, thunder filled the air around them and the rain was blowing sideways.

Barely able to see their own feet, they stumbled across an abandoned hut. It was too wet to start a fire, and they were both exhausted, so they fell fast asleep as soon as they lay down.

In the middle of the night, Wonhyo woke up with a burning thirst. Half asleep, he found a broken bowl full of rainwater. Drinking it down, he gave a sigh and fell back asleep.

In the morning light, Wonhyo was shocked by what he saw: human bones were scattered all around them!

He realized that this was no ordinary hut—it was a plague hut!

Everyone who lived there had died during an epidemic, with no one left to bury the dead. Worse, the "bowl" he'd drunk from was actually half a skull, with flesh still stuck to it.

Running outside, Wonhyo began to vomit as though his insides were coming outside.

Kneeling there with his stomach tied in knots, he suddenly realized, "The water was the same—it's my thoughts that were different. Last night it was pure and refreshing, and now it's so disgusting that I've become ill, yet the only thing that's changed are my thoughts."

As he sat there quietly, Uisang said to him, "Why don't we get going; you'll feel better once we get away from this place."

Wonhyo didn't respond. After a moment he asked Uisang, "Why do you want to go to China?"

"To learn the path, of course."

"The path isn't someplace far away. It's within us, wherever we are. Why go to China to look for what we already have?"

With this, Wonhyo headed back to the lands of Silla.

If you want to discover how things truly work, you'll have to start by looking within yourself.

All of the principles and truths of the universe are already contained within you. Our fundamental mind gives rise to ten thousand different manifestations, and our fundamental mind can combine ten thousand different manifestations into one. This mind that ceaselessly gives rise to things and causes them to subside also causes me to become a thousand different people, and causes all of those people to become one.

So take the functioning of your own mind as your hwadu, your koan. If you do this, you'll come to see your own mind clearly; you'll know what binds your mind, and what frees your mind. You'll discover where you are rich and where you are impoverished, and that it's mind that makes things big, and mind that makes the same things small. You'll know for yourself the unimaginable wonders that this fundamental mind can call forth.

By ceaselessly taking everything that arises through mind as your hwadu, you'll realize that, among all the things in the world, the path to true freedom begins with your own mind—for this is the very place of Buddha.

15. Wisdom Guides the Way

It happened that there was a company where things started to disappear from the warehouse.

The owner of the company was quite adept at both business and managing people, so things had been going nicely. The employees were generally satisfied and there had been no problems with theft before.

Although the value of the missing goods wasn't enormous, the owner wanted to stop the theft before it grew out of hand. So, without telling anyone, he started watching the warehouse after hours.

One night, he saw two people passing boxes out of a side window. The worst part of it was that he recognised the men as two employees that he had always thought highly of. They came from poor backgrounds, but both had always been diligent and seemed completely reliable.

It took a while before he was able to get past his feelings of betrayal and anger, but as he forced himself to carefully think about the situation, he had to admit that the value of what had been stolen wasn't that much.

When he thought about the two men and how hard they had worked for his company, he allowed himself to consider the possibility of extenuating circumstances, so he decided to give them a second chance. If it worked out, he would avoid ruining two men's careers, while keeping two good employees.

The next day, he called both men into his office. "Over the last few weeks, there's been a growing problem with theft from the warehouse. There's no one I trust more than you two, so I'm putting you in charge of the warehouse and solving this problem. Here are the keys."

The two men found themselves in an awkward position. They were so ashamed they could barely look the owner in the face. They felt bad about stealing, but mounting debts had made them desperate.

Now, they heard that they were trusted above all others, and were to be given the keys to the warehouse! They silently resolved to take their responsibility for the warehouse very seriously and become the people the owner thought they were.

They threw themselves into running the warehouse, and came up with several innovations that improved how things were done. Further, the other employees felt that they, too, were trusted, and the company prospered more than ever.

⁎⁎

What would have been the outcome, for the company and the men, if the owner had been fixated on punishing them?

If he had yelled at them and then fired them, it's likely that instead of reflecting upon what they did wrong, they would have started to hate him. And do you know what often happens next? Each side blames the other, raising harmful thoughts and taking advantage of any chance for revenge. Thus it goes, a vicious cycle of despising and trying to hurt each other. When will it end?

In truth, most cases like this can be avoided if those involved are a bit more generous and broad-minded in the beginning. Even a single thought is that important.

The business owner in this story seems to have had a feeling for this. He understood that if you can change the way people think, this is always better than just punishing them. It's better for them and it's better for you. After all, it is mind that moves the body, so instead of punishing the body, he tried to change the mind. He appears to have been someone who unconsciously entrusted everything to the non-dual foundation that connects us all.

Wouldn't it be wonderful to live with this kind of wisdom?

People with this kind of faith in their foundation can't be hurt or overcome by others. Your faith in your foundation causes a spiritual light to grow within the other person, naturally bringing them to repent of their wrongdoings and inspiring them to live a new life. We have to entrust things to our foundation like the company owner entrusted the keys to the two men.

He entrusted everything to them completely. Thus, they felt a sense of empowerment and increased responsibility about their job, and so they focused their energy and ability on doing it well.

However, what if the company owner had spoken about trusting the two men, but in reality was still suspicious of them—always checking up on them, taking back the keys, trying to do the work himself? Most people would say, "Okay, you don't trust me? Do it yourself!" Who could work wholeheartedly in those circumstances?

Your foundation, Juingong, your Buddha-nature, is the one that can truly solve everything, so believe in it to the very end. Entrust everything that confronts you in your daily life to your foundation and have steadfast faith. With true faith, you will never waver.

Never forget that your fundamental mind, your foundation, is a priceless treasure that embraces everything throughout this world and universe.

16. Letting Go

Long ago, in the high mountains of Korea, a traveler was making his way home along a mountain path.

Clouds were drifting between the peaks, and the mountains seemed to vanish into nothingness, only to reappear moments later. At times the clouds would close in and turn his world into just a few misty paces in front of him, with the only sound that of the river far below.

It was all very beautiful, in its own way, and his thoughts turned to his family. No longer paying much attention to the path before him, he stepped a bit too far off the trail; with a sickening rush, the ground gave way under his foot.

Toppling sideways into the abyss, he somehow managed to grab a tree root as he fell. Clinging to it, he tried to pull himself back up, but there was nothing above the root to grab on to.

He was stuck there, hanging on the side of the cliff. The clouds had closed in again and he couldn't see very far, but he heard the river and imagined the long fall to the rocks below.

He gathered his strength and cried out with a wavering voice. "Help! Is anyone there? Help me!"

Amazingly, someone called back, and a moment later an elderly Buddhist nun poked her head out over the cliff.

"Oh thank goodness! Pull me up!" the man cried.

"I'm not strong enough," the nun replied, "but if you just let go, you'll be fine. The ground is right there below you."

"Are you nuts? I can hear the river! I'll be crushed on the rocks—if I don't drown first!"

"No, really!" she told him. "The ground is right below your feet. Just look down."

The man glanced down, but between the heavy fog and his panic, he couldn't see anything.

"There's nothing there! What are you doing, trying to kill me?"

The nun's eyes narrowed. "Listen, you," she said. "You asked me to save you, and now I'm trying. Set aside your fears and let go of that branch. You're just wearing yourself out, clinging and yelling like that. The ground is right there below you."

The nun's reproach gave the man a bit of courage. He was still afraid of falling, but felt a bit less scared.

"Let go? I still can't see anything, but I can't hang here much longer anyway. That nun seems pretty confident that I'll be okay...." With that thought, the man closed his eyes and let go.

In the next instant, he hit soft earth!

The "cliff" he'd been hanging from so desperately was only a few meters high. The whole time, his feet had been dangling just above the ground!

※

What the man was clinging to, and what he let go of, wasn't just the tree root.

Behind his clinging was much more than simply the fear of death. Mixed in with that were all of his attachments to his possessions, his desire for fame and recognition, his disappointments over the things that didn't go well, and of course his concern and love for his family. So you can imagine how much courage it must have taken for him to let go of that branch.

It's a lot easier to talk about letting go than it is to actually do it, especially when it's wrapped up with your family, your children, your pride, and your self-respect. But this letting go is so essential—it is the foundation of all spiritual practices.

Ironically, we're already letting go of every moment. We naturally let go of every moment and go forward. Even with an act as simple as walking, as soon as we take a step, we leave that behind and take another step. Even when we're breathing, as soon as we've finished exhaling, we just naturally inhale. The reason we can let go like this is very simple: because we deeply believe that we can. Not a single cell in your body doubts for an instant that it is possible.

So don't get caught up in "I have to let go." Just know that your foundation, your true self, can completely take care of everything.

Thoroughly trust your foundation. Keep working on this until it becomes as natural as breathing in and breathing out, and you'll know what it means to live a true life!

17. Like a Centipede

A centipede was busily walking along, when a fox called out to it, "Hey, how do you walk so well without your legs getting tangled up? Dozens of legs all going in different directions at the same time, and yet you still walk so smoothly, without once tripping or stumbling. That's incredible!"

The centipede had to agree that it was kind of amazing that he could walk so smoothly. Thinking this, he looked down at his legs, and immediately tripped and fell over.

Lying there on the ground with his legs all tangled up, he was unable to take even a single step forward.

※

Both spiritual practice and daily life go forward like a centipede.

Do you realize all of the things we are doing naturally and automatically at this very instant? You simply drink a glass of water if you're thirsty, sleep if you're tired, and if you're hungry, you get a bite to eat, digest it, and then excrete it.

In the same way, everything inherently arises from your foundation. So just entrust everything back there and go forward. If you can live like this, everything will flow naturally.

Believe in the power and ability that you are inherently endowed with. If you have faith in this foundation and entrust it with everything that arises, then just like food, what's needed will be absorbed, and what needs to be sent out will be sent out. It's exactly like the process of eating and excreting.

However, some people have a hard time trusting that their foundation can do this, and instead try to rely upon their intellect and thoughts to solve the problems they face. But, just like the centipede, those thoughts entangle people and prevent them from moving forward.

18. All by Yourself

It often happens that when a sunim becomes renowned for his or her spiritual practice, the temple that sunim is living at becomes increasingly busy.

Many people come to practice and seek the sunim's guidance. There are visitors everywhere, both genuine practitioners and the merely curious, as well as the spiritual thrill-seekers who come looking for a dazzling experience. There are meals to prepare, ceremonies to attend, guests to look after, and offerings to collect and account for—so it's not exactly the quiet life of tea and meditation that some envision!

One day, the student of such a seon master came to see him. "Sunim, life here is so crowded and busy. It's really interfering with my spiritual practice. With your permission, I'd like to go to somewhere deep in the mountains and find a quiet place where I can practice by myself."

The master studied his student for a moment, and then answered in a quiet voice, "Really? If that's what you want to do, go ahead. There's just one thing though. When you're hungry, don't eat anything that was harvested or prepared by others. Don't accept clothes from other people, and when making your own clothes, don't use fabric made by others.

"If you build a hermitage, don't cut down any trees, and if you're thirsty, don't drink anything. And while traveling, don't step on the ground. If you can do all of these, you have my permission to go and practice by yourself."

The sunim just sat there, stunned. Aside from being utterly impossible, the master's reply was so unexpected.

As the sunim carefully thought about his teacher's words, he realized that his teacher was describing how the world functioned.

"There's nothing in this world that isn't supported by the help of every other thing. Everything in this world lives together, as one life, helping and being helped. 'Go practice by myself.' What on earth could I have been thinking?" He was struck to his very core by this realization.

Afterward, regardless of what the sunim encountered, he always saw that person or situation as another aspect of himself. Their heart was his heart, their behavior was his behavior, and their pain was his pain.

He was very thorough and unceasing in this non-dual practice, and took everything that arose in his life as the subject of his practice.

Eventually, he became deeply enlightened and led innumerable beings to freedom.

⁎⁎⁎

A hut or cave in the mountains isn't a true hermitage. You yourself are a hermitage.

Thus Shakyamuni Buddha said, "You have to escape from your own cave. If you free yourself from the cave of your own mind, then you'll be able to overcome all other hindrances."

If you want to practice spiritual cultivation, don't go looking for a hermitage someplace faraway. Spiritual practice doesn't depend upon some special place, time, or technique. Know that your body, your thoughts, and right here, right now, are the hermitage where you have to practice.

As we've evolved over billions of years, is there any form of life that we haven't been? So how could we look down upon some lives or think that some are precious and others not?

Beings exist with a billion different shapes and sizes, and have just as many different spiritual levels, but fundamentally we all share the same life, the same mind, the same body, work together as one, and share all things among each other—all together, harmoniously, as one.

So, regardless of who you meet or what kind of difficulty you encounter, never see that as something other than yourself. Entrust it all to your foundation.

When we live like this, everything in our life naturally functions together, as one mind, and so we can live freely. It's practicing like this, with what arises in our daily life, that is the essence of true spiritual practice.

19. Three Grains of Millet

Once there was a sunim passing through a village busy with the millet harvest.

He'd been traveling all day and his stomach was looking forward to dinner. Walking by the ripe stalks of millet, he reached out, and touching them, three small yellow grains fell into his hand. He popped them in his mouth without thinking, and kept walking.

Although he immediately forgot all about it, this unconscious act caused the sunim a lot of suffering in his next life. Dying some years later, this karmic debt led him to be reborn as a cow belonging to the farmer whose millet he'd eaten.

For three years he had to work as a cow, and although the farmer was a kind man, life as a cow was still difficult. Not only was the sunim not used to hard physical labor, but he had also retained his human consciousness. He was trapped in a cow's body with all of his human thoughts and feelings, but couldn't communicate with anyone.

Finally, those three long years were nearly finished. Just as the sunim's karmic debt was fulfilled, in the minutes before the cow died, he regained his ability to speak.

He spoke to the kind farmer and explained all of the causes behind his rebirth as a cow. Further, he warned the farmer about a disaster that was approaching the village:

"The day after tomorrow, a gang of five hundred outlaws will attack this village. However, if you prepare meals for all five hundred men, they'll spare the village."

The farmer, amazed by what the cow had said, took it to heart and went to tell the village elders. After much discussion, they gathered the entire village together and began preparing food and places for five hundred men. And then, everyone waited.

As the cow had foretold, two days later five hundred outlaws, bandits of the worst sort, came riding hard into the village.

They'd come expecting the usual thrill of terrified villagers running every which way, but instead, the villagers met them calmly. They announced that they had prepared dinner for all five hundred men, and that if the gentlemen would be seated, they would begin serving them.

"What's going on here? Is this some kind of a trick?" demanded the leader, as he waved his sword around.

The villagers told him about the cow's prophecy, including why the sunim was reborn as a cow. This was just too strange for him to accept. But everyone told him the same story, and as they had provided meals and food for his group, he decided to leave the village intact.

As the days went by, the bandit couldn't help reflecting upon what he had heard about the sunim. Again and again, he found himself comparing the monk's behavior to all the bad things that he himself had done.

In fact, all the outlaws found themselves thinking along the same lines. "If taking three tiny grains of millet can cause a sunim, a disciple of the Buddha, to be reborn as a cow, what will happen to someone like me?"

Each man knew that he had done far more terrible things. Trying to estimate how much they would have to suffer, they were forced to think about how much pain and suffering their actions had caused others.

As a result, the leader and his men began to sincerely repent of the things they had done, and dedicated themselves to learning and applying the teachings of Buddha.

Eventually, all five hundred bandits became Arhats, great beings who extinguished the seeds of desire and anger and transcended birth and death.

⁂

When people hear this story about a sunim becoming a cow because of three grains of millet, they often think this is just a story, something I made up in order to teach them. Of course I tell this story to teach people, but you should know that everything in it actually happened, and that things like this are still happening today.

Nothing in this world happens by accident. A sunim can be reborn as a cow for stealing three grains of millet, and, because of that cow, five hundred bandits can reform and even become Arhats.

Although everything in the world has its own path and its own function, at the same time, it is all interconnected and functioning together as one.

Holding the universe in one hand,
and making it my hat,
hanging the sun and moon from my staff,
with a single step
journeying throughout the soaring mountains.
Everything in these living mountains,
every leaf and pine needle,
are all one body.

Seon Master Daehaeng
February 22, 1986

20. The Same Dream

In a certain village there lived two close friends who were like brothers. They had grown up together, and if you saw one, the other wasn't far away.

One night, one of the friends woke up in a sweat after a strange dream. In it he somehow wound up holding a wide, shallow basket. It seemed trivial, but the image had such an odd feeling that it still bothered him several days later. So, together with his friend, he went to a nearby temple to see the sunim who lived there.

As he explained his dream, the sunim burst out laughing! "Congratulations!" he said. "You're going to be invited to a big party with all kinds of great food.

"This is a good lesson for you—even if a dream seems strange or frightening, always view it positively. Everything depends upon how we use our minds, everything follows our thoughts. So be sure to use your mind in an upright and positive way."

As his friend sat there listening to this, envy began to stir in his heart. "Everything always happens to him! How come things like that never happen to me?" he thought.

As foretold, that afternoon the man received an invitation to a huge party in the neighboring village, and took his friend along. They ate every kind of special food and were completely stuffed by the time they left. But the envy didn't leave the second friend's heart; he was still jealous of his friend's good fortune. Tossing and turning in bed that night, he decided to go see the sunim and pretend to have had the same dream.

"Sunim, you won't believe it, but last night I also dreamed about receiving a wide and shallow bamboo basket. What do you think this means?" he asked the next day.

The sunim's eyes narrowed. "What are you playing at? You'd better be careful—it means you're going to get a real beating."

The second friend couldn't believe his ears; he had described to the sunim the same dream as his friend, but instead of nice words of blessings, all he had gotten were threats.

He went home, grumbling and huffing the whole way. That evening, a number of men from the neighborhood came upon him. When they left, he was lying in his yard, bruised and bleeding.

It happened that he had started a minor rumor about someone as a joke, but the rumor had grown out of all recognition, and he came to be blamed for its final version. Fed up with the rumor and the harm it was causing, some of the men from the village got together to teach him a lesson.

They had really worked him over, and it was four days before he could get out of bed. As he lay there, everything seemed so unfair to him. The original rumor he started was almost harmless, certainly not the sort of thing you would hurt someone for. As for the dream, it never even happened! How could it have predicted him getting beaten up? This really bugged him, so on the fifth day, bruised and aching, he again went to see the sunim.

"Sunim, to tell you the truth, I didn't actually have that dream about the basket. So how could you tell I was going to get beat up?"

The sunim growled at him, "The thoughts you gave rise to became your vision and your destiny. You made up that dream hoping to receive the results of it, and, just as you wanted, you received the results of it: scheming and jealousy."

You see, it wasn't important whether or not he dreamed of a bamboo basket. What mattered was his mind and how he used it.

It makes no difference whether a dream is real or fake, good or bad. This moment we are living in is the combined functioning of both the material and the nonmaterial realms. They function together as one, so the thoughts we raise can change things beyond all imagining.

A dream isn't something that happens only when you are asleep. The thoughts you give rise to while awake also become dreams.

For example, when you see someone who is suffering, and you stop and ask within yourself how you can help, that becomes a good dream. And if you often give rise to those kinds of dreams, good things will result.

On the other hand, if you go around focused only on your own desires, or taking joy in dominating and bothering others, those will also become a dream—a bad one—and those kinds of results will return to you. If you keep this up, you'll find yourself living in a nightmare. The thoughts you've given rise to will follow you around like a bad stink. This is why it is so important to raise thoughts well.

So, like the sunim said, even if you have a horrible dream, don't let yourself think that something terrible is going to happen to you. Turn that thought around.

All of the lives and consciousnesses within your body will follow your thoughts, so instead learn to view things positively and raise kind and generous thoughts.

21. The Good for Nothing Son

Once upon a time, there was an old man who lived with his only son. Unfortunately, his son was the source of every kind of heartache and frustration.

He was always getting drunk and gambling away their money; he often stole from people, and was constantly starting fights. Sometimes he'd scream and rant in the streets, and at other times he'd pass out in a stranger's yard.

His behavior became so outrageous that the old man didn't dare show his face in town.

Not only did the son not take care of his elderly father, one day he even stole the deed to their house. He sold it and spent all the money in a single night on women and alcohol.

Finally the old man exploded: "Get out! Go crawl off and die! Never come back! May the typhus get you for all I care!" Indeed, before long, his son really did catch typhus, and died soon after.

The old man had spoken without thinking, out of deep frustration, but he hadn't really wanted his son to die; it felt as if his sadness and regret would tear his heart into little pieces.

One day a sunim was passing by and saw him sitting in front of his little hut, so sad that no more tears would come.

Seeing the old man's pain, the sunim looked deep inside of the old man. At last he spoke:

"The principles that guide this world function very precisely. They function without even the tiniest error, and nothing happens outside of them. We receive things exactly as we have done them.

"In your last life you wasted all of your family's money on gambling and having fun, and you even sold your own wife. You caused your parents every kind of frustration and heartache, and eventually your father's anger killed him.

"It was this connection that caused him to be reborn as your son. So, who else can you blame for all of this? Your karma from that life was just about to expire, and your son would have straightened out and become an upstanding person. Unfortunately, you couldn't endure this long enough.

"However, losing yourself in sadness won't help either you or your son. If you truly love your son, if you truly want to move past this suffering, then you have to return all of your regrets, anger, and sadness to your foundation. Let go and let go of those.

"Keep doing this, and eventually they will quiet down. It's not easy, but this is the only way forward; this is the only way you can help your son.

"We all share a foundation, our true essence, which is inherently pure and can transform all evil karma and suffering. Through this foundation, we are connected to every animate and inanimate life and object throughout the universe.

"Thus, if you work on returning everything to your foundation, you can also help lift the darkness that is covering your son's mind. So don't be too sad, and don't hate yourself. Let go of all of the bad karma between the two of you, and let go of all the stupid and harmful things that were done.

"When you can let go of those, they will melt down and disappear, helping your son be reborn in a good place." The sunim then said a prayer for the old man's son, and left.

※

Not a single thing in this world remains the same. Everything is ceaselessly flowing and changing.

Even though you or the ones you love suffer from the karma you have created through your words or actions, that suffering can change in an instant, depending upon how well you are able to return thoughts to your foundation, and depending upon the thoughts you give rise to now.

Suppose someone in your family did something truly bad; even in that case, you should unconditionally entrust everything to your foundation. Through it, the minds of parents and children, husbands and wives, and brothers and sisters are all connected as one. So entrust everything to your foundation, Juingong, knowing, "You're the one that can take care of all of this."

For example, if your child runs away and later returns home, don't start yelling at him or her. Instead, embrace them with a warm and gentle heart. Ask them if they are hungry, ask if they were safe.

At first, your child will probably respond in a cold and distant manner, but gradually, as they begin to feel the warmth and love of home, they'll stop wandering around. As you entrust all of your love and concern to your foundation, through their foundation your child will sense those things. In this way, your family will come to share love and happiness together.

This kind of harmony is the source of all good fortune, grace, and virtue.

22. The Travels of a Seon Master

On a cold winter's day, a seon master was traveling through the mountains when he heard a woman sobbing.

The sounds were coming from the area of some graves, and as he went closer he saw a woman sitting on the ground, hugging the body of a young boy. It was the middle of winter, but her clothes were thin and threadbare, and her fingers were torn and bleeding. It looked as if she had been trying to scratch a grave out of the frozen ground.

Through her tears, the woman spoke to her child: "Your father died before you were born, but at least I had you. But now you're gone and I'm all alone. Let's go together. We'll go together and see your father."

Confronted with this situation, the seon master couldn't just continue on his way. From a non-dual state, he asked himself how he could help the woman. Then, as he looked the boy over carefully, he realized that, in terms of karma, the boy had died long before he should have.

The seon master said to the woman, "It wasn't time for your son to die, so if I can find his spirit, he can still return to his body and live. Now listen carefully, this is important: while I'm gone, you have to light a candle so I can find you and your son's body.

"I'm not talking about a physical candle. You need to light the candle of your mind and keep it bright. The deep karmic affinity between the two of you will lead me to your son's body, but if your candle of mind goes out, I won't be able to find my way back to him. And keep your son's body wrapped up and warm."

The child had already been dead for quite a while, so the seon master had to hurry. He sat down, crossed his legs, and immediately entered a state of deep samadhi. He left his body and went to the realms of the dead to look for the boy's spirit.

The first realm he went to was the realm of illusion. After you die, you have to get through the realm of illusion in order to go forward on your own path. But when the seon master arrived, he found this realm absolutely packed with spirits who were stuck there, unable to continue forward.

He told those spirits, "Everything you're seeing now, the terrifying ghosts, the monsters, the writhing snakes, all of these are illusions. They're images created by your consciousness and thus seem real to you. But they're only illusions—just go forward bravely and you'll find that those things have no substance. They'll all disappear."

With this the seon master led all of the spirits through the realm of illusion towards the undying realm.

Those spirits needed to pass through the undying realm in order to reach the realm of birth and death, and so move forward into their next life. However, as the seon master was about to enter, they all suddenly stopped. To them, the undying realm looked like a great ball of fire, and they were afraid of getting burned.

The seon master needed to hurry, but he also couldn't just leave those beings there, so he said to them, "What's before you isn't real; it's just a projection of your mind. You're still thinking in terms of the material realm. You don't have a body now, so there's no way what you see can hurt you."

Understanding this, all of the spirits stepped forward and the flames disappeared. Thus they were able to pass through the undying realm, and so continued on their own paths. The seon master was able to help them move forward because he had become one with them.

Those spirits had been freed, but the seon master still needed to find the boy. He went to the guardian of the undying realm, "I'm looking for the spirit of one who died before his time. Do you know if he's here?"

The guardian looked at his list, but the boy's name wasn't on it. "He's not here, so he must be in the realm of unfinished lives. That's where you need to look."

The seon master went to the realm of unfinished lives, and found that it was filled with those who had died before their proper time. He went to the being who was in charge and together they found the boy's spirit. The seon master quickly led the boy's spirit out of that realm and back to the realm of the living.

In the meantime, the boy's mother had been working very hard to keep her candle of mind bright, but she was tiring.

Her light had almost gone out when the seon master arrived back at the boy's body. As soon as the boy's spirit touched his body, his heart started to beat and with a great gasp he began to breathe again.

His mother burst into tears, holding her son to her chest as she knelt there. Looking at them, the seon master put his hands together and bowed, and then continued on his way.

Our mind has no substance, so it can't be caught or trapped by anything. It's free to function and do whatever is needed.

However, people have evolved with a physical body for so many eons that even when they're dead, they think their existence is subject to the laws of the material realm.

So, even though they don't have a body, they think fire can hurt them. Even though their minds can go anywhere instantly, they try to walk or look for a car or train to take them where they want to go. They think that snakes can bite them and knives can stab them. In truth, none of those things have any power over them.

Nevertheless, the thinking done while living in the material realm becomes thought habits that tend to bind people. Even after death, these habits constrain and hinder them.

If you want to be able to go forward after death without being caught by these kinds of illusions, then you have to let go of your discriminations while alive. However, you'll probably find times when your expectations and ideas about how things should be cause you to become angry or offended by something that was ultimately quite minor.

Likewise, there are probably also times when you're able to shrug off things that are quite difficult and painful, all the while striding forward with confidence and determination. You're able to do that because, even though you didn't realize it, you were discarding your fixed ideas and entrusting everything to your foundation.

When you can entrust everything to your foundation in this way—the big things, the small things, everything—you'll free yourself in this life, as well as the next.

And, like the seon master, you will be able to save not just yourself, but everyone else you encounter as well.

23. Even a Tree Understands Gratitude

Long ago, a well-to-do man brought home a tree sapling. He planted it in the center of his courtyard and took care of it himself.

Year after year, the man fussed over the tree, protecting it from insects and giving it just the right amount of water and fertilizer. And year after year, the tree showered the courtyard with magnificent flowers.

One night, the man had a strange dream in which the tree was talking to him. It told him that a great disaster would soon strike, so he needed to leave the area right away. But the man didn't take it seriously, and forgot all about it by the time he sat down for breakfast.

Three days later, all of the man's animals broke out of their corrals and pens and ran away. His servants looked everywhere, but they couldn't find a single one. He stomped around cursing his bad luck, for now it looked as though he wasn't going to be well-to-do for much longer!

Finally, exhausted by his emotions, he fell into a deep sleep. Again the tree appeared to him, imploring him to leave:

"A volcano is about to erupt! There is no time. You must leave immediately! I'm going too!"

This time, the man took the dream seriously. As he left his house, he noticed that the tree's leaves had already started to wilt.

He ordered his family and servants to hurriedly pack their belongings, and then he ran out to warn everybody who lived in the area. They all left in a great rush and headed for a valley several miles away. Arriving, they were shocked to see all of the animals that had run away.

As they stared at the animals, a series of huge explosions shook the ground. The ground rocked like it was water, and day turned to night.

Several days later, after things had calmed down, the man was looking over a wasteland of ash and boulders. A few crushed walls were all that was left of his home.

Even a plant that seems to know nothing sends down deeper roots in a year when typhoons will come.

How can we human beings, who are endowed with the six senses and who have evolved through so many levels of existence, know less than a plant? We human beings have more abilities than plants or animals, yet how is it that we don't perceive what is right under our noses?

Why is this? It's because we don't see our foundation, our inherent mind, which has existed before we were born. Instead we've only seen what our eyes have shown us.

We must start by having faith in our foundation, our true nature. Then reality will become clearer and our wisdom will grow brighter. We'll also become able to freely use the abilities inherent within us.

Believe in your foundation. It's this foundation, your true self, that can show you how to become free.

24. The Pure-hearted Sculptor

If you go to Bulguk Temple near Gyeongju, you can still see in the courtyard two magnificent stone pagodas. There is an air about them of something profound and peaceful, and perhaps you will understand why when you hear how they came to be.

Over a thousand years ago, after Kim Daesung became prime minister of the Silla Kingdom, he began to rebuild Bulguk Temple.

He wanted to add two pagodas that would express the richness and depth of the Buddha's teachings, but in order to do this he knew he needed to find an artisan whose great skill was matched by an equally deep sincerity and faith. Unfortunately, no matter how hard he looked, he couldn't find such a person.

Yet Kim Daesung knew that if he was sincere enough, he would surely find a craftsman who was equally sincere.

So, for one hundred days, he fasted and prayed. Although he was rebuilding Bulguk Temple in honor of his parents, it wasn't for them alone that he was praying. He was praying for all beings, that they would truly awaken to their inherent Buddha-nature, and that the entire world would live together peacefully and harmoniously.

He poured his entire heart into his prayers and meditation, and on the night of the one hundredth day the Buddha appeared in a dream, saying to him, "In the lands of the old Baekje kingdom is a sculptor of great depth and sincerity, called Asadal."

Kim Daesung left immediately for the southwest of Korea, to the lands that had been the old Baekje kingdom. He spent months there, traveling through villages and cities, always asking if anyone had ever heard of a stone carver by the name of Asadal.

One day, as he traveled through a remote mountain valley, he heard a woman call, "Asadal, dinner's ready." At last, he had found the man he'd been looking for!

He humbly asked Asadal to design and carve two pagodas for Bulguk Temple, and explained his hope that they would express the Buddha's teachings and guide all who gazed upon them.

Asadal was filled with joy at the prospect of being able to contribute to the reconstruction of a great temple like Bulguk, but he couldn't immediately accept Kim Daesung's offer.

For Asadal had a wife, Asanyo, who he loved very much. They lived together with her father, and it was he who had taught Asadal all of the stone carver's arts. But he was elderly, and would never survive the journey to Bulguk Temple.

Yet if Asadal went by himself, Asanyo would be left trying to care for her father by herself. No matter how Asadal looked at the situation, there seemed to be no good answer.

That night Asadal told his wife about Kim Daesung's proposal. Asanyo was filled with joy, for she loved him deeply and knew that he was capable of producing something wonderful. But she noticed that Asadal was uneasy, and also realized that even traveling to Bulguk Temple would take many, many weeks.

"I know the circumstances will be difficult, but the pagodas you'll make will convey the Buddha's teachings throughout the centuries. Don't worry about father; I'll take good care of him. And even though we'll be apart, think of all the benefits those pagodas will have for so many generations of people.

"You've dreamed about being able to do something like this, and when the work is finished, we can be together again."

With this, Asadal made up his mind to go to Bulguk Temple and carve the pagodas. He and Asanyo held each other and cried for a long time, promising that one day they would hold each other again.

After he arrived at Bulguk temple, Asadal set about designing and carving the pagodas. Although he missed Asanyo terribly, everything he did was imbued with the love he felt for her.

Thinking of her hope that these pagodas would benefit generation after generation, his great love for her expressed itself as compassion for all beings and the hope that they would dissolve all traces of self-centeredness and awaken to the eternal, fundamental Buddha within.

He focused on the pagodas with this utter sincerity, and the hope that they would be beacons that would guide all beings to this bright path.

When Asadal began to work on the first pagoda, called the Dabo Pagoda, an image of the four all-embracing virtues arose within him, for with these, anyone would be able to live a true life and would open themselves to innumerable blessings.

The first virtue is freely giving to those in difficulty. The second is encouraging others to live together harmoniously through gentle speech and a kind face. The third virtue is helping others through words, actions, and even mind. And the fourth virtue is sharing unconditionally, by becoming one with other people and their circumstances.

Asadal decided to represent these virtues as pillars, so after finishing the foundation of the pagoda, he erected four rectangular pillars, plain looking but sturdy.

On top of these he built an elaborate and refined structure, representing the functioning of the earth and heavenly realms. Thus, the Dabo Pagoda teaches us that it is these four virtues that support the functioning of all things in the world and universe.

As Asadal designed and carved the second pagoda, known as the Sokga Pagoda, it was with the hope that beings would put into practice the four all-embracing virtues represented by the Dabo Pagoda, and in so doing, they would awaken to their inherent nature and go on to become Buddhas themselves.

This he represented with clean, straight lines and smooth squares, one on top of another; thus developed the Sokga Pagoda's noble form. Even today, these pagodas are still there, speaking silent words to all who come.

Both Kim Daesung and Asadal were deeply sincere people, who worked hard at letting go of self-centeredness and the tendency to see themselves as existing apart from others.

Kim Daesung wanted to build the pagodas in order to help all beings, while Asadal entrusted every single thing to his inherent nature, and every stroke of his chisel contained his pure heart. And so, the Dabo Pagoda and the Sokga Pagoda are made of much more than just stone.

If people realized just how precious it is to be born as a human being, they wouldn't waste their life just wandering around.

Even worse than this are those who think only of themselves, and so turn their backs upon the tremendous opportunities to create virtue and merit which come from being born as a human being. The thoughts we are giving rise to now can even determine whether we are reborn as a more evolved human being, or whether we wear the mask of an animal.

So, have a great heart like Kim Daesung, and raise an intention to benefit each and every being. Diligently rely upon your foundation with the sincerity and focus of Asadal.

Practice like this, and your life will shine forth like the Dabo and Sokga Pagodas, whose light remains undiminished after even a thousand years.

25. The Scholar and the Regent

Long ago there was a poor scholar who, as it turned out, was a distant relation to the all-powerful regent of Korea.

One season, an occasion came about to make a rare trip to the capital. It was the tradition in those days that when visiting distant places, travelers would greet relatives who lived in the area. It didn't have to be anything fancy, just a bow and a few words, but to skip this would have been unthinkable for a person of good upbringing.

So, after arriving in Seoul, the scholar set out to greet his famous relative. The regent lived on a large estate, where he guided the affairs of the country. It was almost a palace, with many residences and offices surrounded by a great wall.

Approaching the guards, the scholar explained why he was there, and after some time he was admitted to the complex. He'd worn his best clothes, but even those were a bit shabby and had been mended more than once. "Another poor, country relative," grinned the court literati.

He was given a room in the lesser guest quarters, which were really not much better than servants' quarters, and told to wait. Day after day he waited. Finally the call came.

Striding into the audience room, he gave a dignified bow before the regent. The regent, however, appeared to be discussing some important matter with one of his aides and didn't seem to have noticed the scholar. So the scholar bowed a second time.

In the next instant, the regent exploded, "What do you think you're doing! Are you wishing me dead?"

You see, in Korea, people bowed once to a living person, twice to a dead person at memorial services, and three times to the Buddha or a holy person. So bowing twice to someone was very offensive, almost like cursing them.

The scholar was in hot water now. The regent had a bad reputation, and those who fell afoul of him tended to meet an unpleasant end. But the scholar didn't shrink back, and instead responded with confidence and a smile.

"Your Excellency has perhaps misunderstood my intention. I bowed once when I entered, but as you seemed quite busy with other matters, I bowed once more in farewell."

He smiled again at the regent, "With your leave then, I'll be going. Goodbye." And then he left.

The regent just sat there, stunned for a moment. He was the most powerful man in all Korea, yet this country scholar with the shabby clothes had got the better of him.

After a bit, the regent gave a reluctant smile, and ordered a servant to bring the scholar back.

"You have some kind of nerve. Thinking I didn't see you trying to get my attention, and then playing games with me! But you remained calm and had a lot of guts to answer me like that.

"I need people like that, who can jump into a task with courage and an upright demeanor. Therefore, I'm putting you in charge of military training for your home district. See that the soldiers are properly trained, and develop good leaders."

For the scholar, this was an unexpected blessing, because it was an important position with a good income attached to it. It also provided entry into the upper ranks of the civil service, and the opportunity to help many, many people. In fact, it completely changed the fortunes of his family.

We, too, can live with the same upright dignity, courage, and wisdom as that scholar.

All you have to do is learn to believe in your foundation. Then, regardless of what kinds of circumstances you find yourself in, you can respond calmly and naturally, with courage and dignity.

In appearance, we can be divided into men and women, and by our different roles. But in our fundamental mind there is no male or female, old or young. So, regardless of who you are, if your faith in your foundation is unshakable, you'll be able to entrust everything to it.

In so doing, you will be able to take care of everything throughout heaven and earth.

26. Bodhidharma's Sandal

The first patriarch of Chan (Seon) in China came from India and was called Bodhidharma.

One day he came across a huge snake coiled up in the middle of a path. It was so big that he couldn't walk around it, and it wouldn't budge even an inch. Bodhidharma saw that the snake was intensely cultivating its mind in order to be reborn as a human being, but he knew that if the snake was startled, in a moment of panic it could kill someone.

Bodhidharma saw what he had to do. His mind left his body and entered the snake; becoming one with the snake, he led it far away to a place where it could practice in peace, without risk to anyone else.

However, when he returned to where he had left his body, it was gone! Someone had taken his body, which was quite nice, as bodies go. Left in its place was the body of a fat, ugly man, who looked like a bandit.

Without a body, Bodhidharma wouldn't be able to help unenlightened beings, so he had no choice but to use the body that was there, even though it was so completely different from his original body. This is why he looks so ugly in paintings!

Because Bodhidharma was such an enlightened master who could freely manifest as needed, even

King Wu of the Yang Dynasty would ask him for advice.

One day, the king said to him, "I've made huge offerings of food and clothing to the Sangha, and I've built many temples. Can you tell me how much virtue and merit I've accumulated?"

What he was really asking was what his reward would be. Bodhidharma answered him, "Nothing. You haven't created any virtue or merit at all."

The king was deeply stung by this. His shock turned to resentment, which began to fester and grew into hatred. In the end, he ordered his men to poison Bodhidharma. This they did, and Bodhidharma was buried in the temple where he had taught for so many years.

One day, the king's envoy was returning from a diplomatic mission to India. On the way home, he met Bodhidharma!

The master was walking toward the west, carrying a staff with one sandal hanging from it. The envoy hadn't heard about Bodhidharma's death, and greeted him warmly, inquiring where he was bound for.

"Oh, I'm heading west. I'm going back to the place I came from," answered the great master.

Later, when King Wu heard about this, he was stunned. "What happened? He drank poison and died!" The king ordered Bodhidharma's grave dug up, and in the grave was one sandal, nothing else.

✻

The story of Bodhidharma teaches us three very deep principles.

The first is the principle, or truth, of non-duality. "A thief is my shape, a handsome man is my shape, and a snake is also my shape."

This is how Bodhidharma viewed the world because he completely understood that nothing was separate from himself. Everyone and everything he met was another shape of himself. If Bodhidharma had been full of thoughts of "I," he couldn't have entered the snake and saved it.

The second deep truth of this story is that even as we experience life and death, ultimately we are not born, nor do we die.

Although King Wu had Bodhidharma killed, there was never a moment when Bodhidharma died. From the very beginning, there has never been a thing called "I" that could die. In an instant, we change our shape and go, and in an instant, we change our shape and reappear in this world.

We're only changing our shape. "Bodhidharma coming to the east and returning to the west" refers to this process of dying and being born. You should know that we go through death and birth just like we walk up the stairs and down the stairs.

The third deep principle of this story is that of doing without doing.

When the king gave offerings, he needed to do it while letting go of any thoughts of giving. Only then could his act of giving become virtue and merit capable of saving the king, as well as the people of the nation.

True virtue and merit is possible when you do things without the thought of "I did something." Then, there's nothing you've done, and nothing you haven't done.

It was this principle of doing without any thought of doing that Bodhidharma was teaching the king. By teaching one man, the leader of the country, Bodhidharma had been trying to help all the people of the nation.

The sandal in the grave was left there to show that within each one of us there is a "fundamental self," or a foundation, through which everything in the universe is combined together as one. Our existence is the manifestation of this foundation, and that's the meaning of Bodhidharma having one sandal hanging from his staff.

Our life itself is like someone walking with a staff over their shoulder, and a sandal hanging from it. The political realm is no different. When we can put one sandal in the heavens and one on the ground, beneficial policies and leadership will be the result.

If those who wish to lead carry around thoughts of "me" and "I'm doing," they won't be able to govern properly, nor will their actions result in any merit or virtue for the land.

27. It's Hard to Say

Long ago in China, there lived an old man who raised horses. One day, his most prized horse, a magnificent stallion, ran away.

His friends and neighbors came by to console him, saying what a shame it was to lose such a fine animal. But the old man didn't seem particularly bothered. In fact, he spoke as if nothing much had happened.

"Well, it's hard to say. If you have something, eventually it has to leave, doesn't it? And when something goes, something else comes, doesn't it?"

Sure enough, a few days later the stallion returned, and brought with him a truly magnificent mare. Everyone could tell that this horse was something special.

"Hey, congratulations! Instead of losing a horse, you gained a beautiful new one! What luck!"

But the old man was unmoved. "It's hard to say. When you gain something, you often lose something else, so there's no point in getting too excited about it."

Sometime later, the old man's son was riding the mare when he was thrown off and broke his leg. They set his leg as best they could, but it was clear the son was going to have a bad limp for the rest of his life. With his only son crippled, people expected the old man to be shattered, and tried to console him.

However, he surprised them again: "It's hard to say. There might be some good in this somewhere."

A few years later, the country was plunged into a series of endless civil wars. In the chaos that followed, one of the contending armies came through the village and took away all of the young men—except one.

There was one young man with a bad limp who they left behind.

※

Gain and loss are like two sides of one coin—you can never have one without the other.

Most people devote so much energy to celebrating gain and mourning loss; however, if you understand that they always go together, you won't get caught up in either of them.

The old man knew that these always go hand in hand, so regardless of huge gains or terrible losses, he was always able to remain calm and centered. He wasn't filled with delight at an unexpected windfall, and a sudden loss didn't plunge him into despair. Isn't this a wise way to live?

If you think deeply about the joy and sadness people feel about gain and loss, you will realize that these arise from greed. And greed itself is caused by ignorance.

How do you want to live your life? If you want to live wisely, with clear insight, you have to start with letting go. Entrust everything you encounter, along with all of the emotions arising within you, to your foundation.

The ability of your foundation is vast beyond imagining. No matter how much you take from it, it will never run out. No matter how much you put into it, it can take all of it in without missing a thing. It can become as big as the universe or as small as the point of a needle. At the level of your foundation, important or unimportant and good or bad do not exist. It is the place where everything dissolves and disappears, and the place that sends forth everything into this world.

Thus, if you can keep returning everything to this place, then even though you haven't awakened and don't understand how things truly work, you'll be less and less caught by the good and bad things that confront you, and you'll find yourself taking the middle way in whatever circumstances arise.

28. Mother-in-law Saves the Family

In the city of Wonju there was a woman who sold bean sprouts in the market. She and her young son were quite poor, and life seemed like an endless cycle of just scraping by.

The burdens of poverty can often make a person ruthless or hopeless, but throughout it all the woman remained kind and upright. Further, through her behavior and the stories she told, her son also absorbed those qualities.

Her heartfelt desire was to see her son live a life free of poverty and hardship. Thus, she worked every single day in the market, in the rain and in the snow, and in this way she put her son through college.

Upon graduation, he immediately landed a very good job, and not long afterwards married a nice girl. She too came from a poor family, but had a good heart. He bought a house where they could live with his mother, and together the three of them were happy.

Although his mother was now living with her married, successful son, she didn't want to be a burden to him or his wife, so most days she still sold bean sprouts in the market.

About six months later, her son's company sent him to work on a project in the Middle East. He was to be there for nearly two years, and his wife had to stay behind.

Home alone for most of the day, the hours weighed heavily on his wife. One day when her friends were visiting, she wound up playing a popular card game called *hwatu* for the first time. The time flew by as they played, betting pocket change as mini-fortunes were won and lost.

This was how it started for her; gradually she began playing for increasing stakes. She had been receiving most of her husband's pay, together with his overseas bonuses, and it was enough to have been able to save a decent amount. But before long she was pouring it all into her gambling habit.

Her mother-in-law realized what was happening, but no matter how she scolded or tried to persuade her daughter-in-law, it made no difference—the young wife was completely addicted to gambling. Unable to sit by and watch, her mother-in-law moved out.

About a year later, the son returned to Korea a few months sooner than expected, and his wife panicked. Not only had she gambled away all of the money she was supposed to be saving, but she didn't even know what had become of her mother-in-law.

Desperate, she lied to her husband. "Your mother just moved out one day. I wasn't home, and I looked everywhere, but couldn't find her," she said, her voice trailing off. "I didn't tell you because I knew you'd worry."

Her husband stormed out and went to the market, where he started looking up his mother's old friends. He eventually found her, and when he brought her home, his wife fell to her knees and begged her husband's forgiveness.

Unexpectedly, her mother-in-law turned to her son and said that his wife hadn't done anything wrong. Instead, she'd left because she didn't like being cooped up and wanted to be near her friends in the market.

Not only that, a few minutes later, when her son wasn't looking, she gave her daughter-in-law a bankbook with the daughter-in-law's name on it. It showed a sizable amount of money in the account, enough that her husband wouldn't think twice about it.

When her mother-in-law had left the house, she'd already thought out a plan. She rented the cheapest backroom available, and then, while continuing to sell bean sprouts, she did every other kind of odd job she could find. She lived like this for a year, saving every penny she could, because she didn't want to see her son's family break apart.

The wife realized what her mother-in-law must have gone through to save that kind of money, and it was a life-changing event for her. She hugged her mother-in-law, awed by such unbelievable kindness, and it was a long time before her tears stopped.

※

What would have happened if the mother-in-law had let herself give in to frustration and resentment? Could things have turned out this well?

If you dislike someone and carry around harsh thoughts toward them, ultimately you are the one who will suffer the most. So, in all of the things you do, and in dealing with the things that confront you, maintain a kind and gentle frame of mind.

No matter how angry or betrayed you feel, do your best to avoid speaking or acting rashly. Think about the situation from the other person's perspective, and deeply reflect upon your own behavior and assumptions.

This is the wisdom that can change the world. If you can live with this kind of wisdom, how could your family and society not become happy and peaceful?

A single, tiny thought can change the world. This is why I'm often telling you that everything begins with the thoughts one person gives rise to. So can there be anyone whose thoughts don't matter?

29. The Man with Two Sets of Parents

A thousand years ago or more, in the Korean kingdom of Silla, there lived a husband and wife who were servants to a nobleman. Thus, by birth, their son was also a servant.

One day during a typhoon, the husband went out to ensure that their master's fields weren't being washed away. While checking the dikes, he was swept away by a raging stream and drowned.

The nobleman was a kind-hearted person, and couldn't help reflecting on his servant's many years of service. The man had always worked hard, taking care of whatever needed to be done. It didn't matter if it wasn't his job, nor did he avoid the difficult jobs or leave his work for others to do.

As the nobleman considered his servant's many contributions, he decided to give the man's son a large piece of farmland. With this land the son would never again have to work for anyone else. But to the nobleman's surprise, although the son gratefully accepted the land, he continued to show up for work every day, all the while still taking good care of his mother.

Several months later, a sunim passed by collecting donations for a temple. As the son listened to him chanting, something stirred deep within him. He decided to give the sunim the entire piece of land in the name of his father.

His mother tried to dissuade him, saying, "What about your future? This land is your chance for a better life."

The son replied, "I was given this land because of father's sacrifice, so now I think it should be used for his benefit."

His mother was still uneasy, but was consoled by the knowledge that his good heart and the virtue of his actions would take care of him. However, unexpectedly, her son became ill and died three days later.

As for the sunim who had received the land, he was no ordinary monk. He was a great practitioner who had deeply awakened. He had been impressed by the young man, and perceived that he had a deep and pure mind.

The sunim wanted the young man to have a bright future, but there was no ordinary way the sunim could help him—under the laws of those days, the young man was born into the lowest level of society, and could never rise above that. So, after much reflection, the sunim used his deep spiritual ability to help the young man to leave his old life and body behind.

Next, the sunim appeared in the dream of a high-ranking minister who despaired of ever having children. In the dream, the sunim said, "In the village of Moryang, a young man called Daesung has died today, but in the near future he will be born again as your child. Raise him well, for he will grow up to become a great and virtuous leader."

The minister had this same dream for three nights in a row. It was quite an odd dream, and he was curious about it, so finally he sent a servant to investigate the events mentioned in his dreams. Amazingly, the servant reported that in fact, in a remote village called Moryang, a man named Daesung had recently died.

Knowing this, the minister wasn't too surprised when his wife became pregnant a few months later. She gave birth to a healthy baby boy, and everyone in the family was so excited for them. After so many years of no children, at last, a healthy son!

However, as the midwife was washing the baby, she realized that his left hand was clenched in a fist and wouldn't open. In a hurried whisper she called for the minister.

The new father's stomach turned to ice at the news, and he rushed into the room; but as he touched his son's clenched fist, it gently opened as if it were the petals of a flower. There, in the palm of his hand, was a name written in letters of glowing gold: Daesung, or "Great Protector."

His parents gave him their family name "Kim," and raised him well. In fact, he eventually grew up to become prime minister of the Silla Kingdom, and under his wise guidance Silla enjoyed peace and prosperity for many decades.

When Kim Daesung was old enough, he went looking for his mother from his past life. He brought her to live with his mother from this life, and took good care of both of them.

He had deeply experienced the truth that everything is constantly changing and manifesting, with nothing remaining fixed or unchanging.

Furthermore, he saw the suffering that people experienced from not knowing this, so to help them understand, and to honor his parents from both lives, he built two great Buddhist centers, Bulguk Temple and Sokgul Hermitage.

Once when Shakyamuni Buddha was traveling, he suddenly stopped and bowed to a large pile of bones that was beside the road.

When his disciples asked him why he'd done that, he pointed at the bones and explained:

"Although we were born with the body of a human being, this hasn't always been the case. On the way to becoming human beings, we've lived as every kind of being imaginable, with parents and children, sisters and brothers. Having passed through eons, is there any being that wasn't your mother or father, your son or daughter?"

If you've awakened to your true self, then you may realize just how many different shapes you've had. If you truly know this, if you truly understand how many times you've switched places, how many times every other shape has been your shape, then how could other lives not be just as precious as your own?

In this life and all our lives up until now, we have had parents and children, brothers and sisters. Is one set more precious than the others?

All beings are our mother and father, our son and daughter, so we need to treat everyone with this much respect and value.

30. The King and the Blacksmith

Once there was a king who wanted to see for himself how his people were living, so he dressed like an ordinary merchant and traveled throughout the country.

As he walked past a house early one morning, he heard a man say, "It's so cold today! What a miserable morning! Generation after generation we suffer like this, repaying debts above and giving light below." The king saw that the man was a blacksmith, talking to himself as he worked to get a fire started in his forge.

Try as the king might, he couldn't understand what the blacksmith had meant by this.

Once he returned to his palace, the king sent for the blacksmith and asked him the meaning of his words. The blacksmith gave a huge sigh of relief. He'd thought he was in deep trouble, because he couldn't imagine why anyone in the palace would want to see someone like him!

Doing his best to keep from trembling, he answered the king, "I come from a long line of blacksmiths. My father was one, as was my grandfather. It's hard work, and hot in the summers, but I can't really complain, because I've been able to feed my family and see that my children can marry well.

"That said, every single night I have to worry about the forge. If the fire goes completely out, so that even the embers die, it's often midday before I can get the fire started and hot enough to work with. So, every night I have to add wood to it, and every morning I have to get up at sunrise and feed the fire before it dies.

"On the morning you passed by, it was very cold out and the fire had already died, so I was asking myself why I had to suffer like that. Well, I realized that I go through these hardships in order to take care of my parents and grandparents, and to raise my sons and daughters, all seven of them.

"I owe a huge debt to my parents who gave birth to me and worked so hard to take care of me. And I know that plants won't grow with just water: they also need sunlight.

"So I was thinking that I have to give light to my children as well as food and clothing. That's why I was grumbling that it's so hard to repay the debts I owe above and to give light below."

Hearing this, the king felt like he had finally remembered something he had forgotten a long time ago. Slapping his knee, he exclaimed,

"Every word you said is the truth. Nothing is separate, everything is connected together, even those who have died or are yet to be born. Each has their own role, yet they also work altogether as a whole."

The king saw clearly that there was not the least difference between him and the blacksmith. He realized that the purpose of wearing a crown was not to indulge himself and live as comfortably as possible, enjoying the benefits of money and power.

Like the blacksmith who took care of his parents and gave light to his children, the king also had a role to play. Above, it was his job to ensure that the country was prosperous and strong, and below, he was responsible for ensuring that the people were well fed and that virtue prospered.

None of these things should be tainted by the attitude of "Look at what I've done." Rather, these were things that the king had to do purely because he was born as a human being; being a king only increased the extent of his responsibilities.

Out of gratitude to the blacksmith, the king gave him a large farm with many servants. Guided by his newfound wisdom, the king ruled so well that the entire country prospered and lived in peace.

⁂

No matter how many good deeds you've done or how much you've given, if you still carry around thoughts such as "I did that," then your actions won't produce true virtue or merit.

Furthermore, the material and the non-material have to be included together, such that if you move even a single finger, it can support the entire universe. Then whatever you do will truly become virtue and merit.

When you can do this, you can feed all beings with a single bowl of rice: though you have just one bowl, the rice will never run out.

Because the world truly works like this, when you take care of your parents and children, do it while knowing they are not separate from yourself, and while letting go of any thoughts that involve "I'm doing." If you can do this, harmony will pervade your entire family.

31. The Examination

During the Joseon Dynasty, there was a scholar who was on his way to Seoul to take the national civil service examination.

He had been walking all day under the late summer sun, and was hungry and tired. Seeing an inn, he entered its courtyard and sat down on the raised platform with a heavy sigh. He ordered food and drink, and as he took out his purse, he found himself staring at it with tears in his eyes.

The tears welled up because while he had spent the last several years studying for the civil service test, his wife had been the one who supported their family.

Although she belonged to the nobility, she worked in other people's kitchens and took in their sewing and mending. One copper coin at a time, she supported her husband and children, and saved enough for her husband's traveling expenses.

What made it worse was that this wasn't the first time the scholar had taken the national examination; it was famously difficult, and he had already failed it several times. So, as he looked at the coins in his purse, he felt the weight of his wife's love and how bravely she had gone about taking care of the family.

For several years, the entire country had been gripped by a drought. If the rains did come, it was always as floods that washed away entire fields, or buried them under sand and gravel. Words can't express how much the ordinary people suffered.

But the worst disaster of all was the behavior of the corrupt and greedy officials that plagued so many areas. Even when the people were one step away from eating boiled grass and tree bark, these officials still insisted that they pay their taxes, and they would take every last thing of value a family possessed.

If the local officials had just reported the situation to the king, he would have waved the taxes in the districts that were suffering. But then the officials would have lost the chance to steal part of the tax money. So they kept quiet and the people continued to suffer.

Thus, the scholar couldn't pass through a single village, no matter how small, without hearing the sounds of weeping or the groans of the sick and dying. He vowed, "If I pass that test with a high score, I'm going to become a royal inspector, and I will not let the people be abused and suffer like this!"

You see, in those days the king had secret inspectors whose job it was to tell him what was really going on in the country. In addition, they had the authority to solve any injustice on the spot. All of the soldiers and police had to obey the inspector instantly. These inspectors could even have officials arrested, exiled, and beaten to within an inch of their lives.

The most terrifying sight a corrupt official could see was a shabby peasant suddenly calling out in a fearsome voice and holding high the badge of a king's inspector. Even the most cunning and powerful official's blood would turn to ice at the sight of that round, brass badge with its image of five horses. These inspectors truly had the power to relieve people's suffering.

As the scholar thought of the suffering of so many people and of his wife, he sat up straight, drew his shoulders back, and growled, "I'll pass that examination or die trying!"

As he wiped the tears from his eyes, a weary old man sat down beside him. "Oh my legs! And if it were any hotter today, I don't know what I'd do." Smiling at the scholar, he asked, "Where are you off to on a day like this?"

"I'm heading up to the capital to take the national examination."

"Well then," said the old man, "you'd better take a look at this." Out of his backpack he took an old book and gave it to the scholar.

The scholar opened it up, but as he looked through it, he saw that every page in the book was blank. He turned to speak to the old man, but no one was there; the old man had vanished.

"Had he been there at all?" wondered the scholar. "Perhaps I'm suffering from heatstroke?" But no, the book the old man had given him was still in his hands.

He sat there for a long time looking at the blank pages of that book. Passers-by saw him and imagined that he was studying some particularly difficult text, and yet not a single word was written on those pages.

Suddenly the scholar gave a shout. "Hah! Who would have guessed! There's nothing here, so it can become one with everything, and can manifest as anything. It contains everything in the world. If one takes that as their center, they can hold all the realms of existence and non-existence in the palm of their hand."

The scholar reverently put the book in his bag, and with a smile on his face continued on his way to the capital.

On the day of the exam, he went to the palace and found his seat. At last, the instructors revealed the examination topic: the word "Everything." Everyone had to compose an essay or poem with "everything" as their subject.

The scholar thought of the book the old man had given him, with its blank, white pages, and smiled as he began to write about the principle by which everything in the universe functions.

Needless to say, his poem received the highest scores. He met the king, who upon hearing his story made him a royal inspector and charged him with protecting the people and upholding justice.

※

When peas are immature, they tend to stick to the pod, don't they? However, when they have completely ripened, they burst out with just a touch of the fingers.

The scholar's study of human virtue and how we should live had ripened to the point where those blank pages alone were enough to open his eyes. Everyone needs to reach this point.

There are so many teachings left by great practitioners; however, if your own spiritual practice isn't deep enough, those teachings will remain just words on a page. Even though you're not yet at the stage of understanding the blank page, do your best to at least correctly understand the true meaning of the written words. If you can't understand even the written words, how will you be able to pass the examination?

But when your practice has deepened and matured, then without even a single word, you will understand the ultimate meaning.

32. Carrying a Sheep on Your Shoulders

A long time ago in India, a man was on his way to the temple to offer a sheep to the gods.

He had tied its legs together and was carrying it over his shoulders. It was very heavy, but at that time, a sheep was the best possible offering one could make, so the man felt quite proud of what he was doing.

He was taking heavy steps, covered in sweat, when he happened to pass a priest. The priest turned to him and said, "Why on earth are you carrying a piglet on your shoulder? You know, that's not really a proper offering. Why don't we roast it and eat it here, and later when you're able, you can make a proper offering."

The man just stood there, without saying a word, so the priest turned and left.

Actually, the man was stunned. Many thoughts went through his mind, most of which were along the lines of, "'Not really a proper offering?' 'A piglet?' He's lost his mind. Can't he see that I'm carrying a sheep?"

Shaking his head, he continued on his way. You could almost follow the trail left by the drops of his sweat. The sun beat down on him and his steps became shorter and shorter as the sheep seemed to get ever heavier. But as he thought of the precious offering he carried, he redoubled his effort. Still, he was annoyed every time he thought about the word "piglet"!

He'd been walking for a while when he met another priest. He didn't expect great words of praise, but a smile or a word of encouragement would have been welcome. Do you think this is what he heard?

No. If you can believe it, the priest said, "Why are you carrying a dog on your back? Let's take it down to the village and they'll cook it up nicely for us. It'd be a bit embarrassing to offer the gods a dog, wouldn't it?"

This time the man exploded. "Have you all lost your minds? Can't you see that I'm carrying a sheep? Do you have any idea how expensive it was? You must be blind to look at such a first rate sheep and call it a dog!"

The priest looked at man with an expression that said he had no idea why the man was upset.

"If you don't want to go cook this dog, that's fine, too." And then the priest continued on his way.

The man just stood there, unable to believe what he was hearing. "Everybody's gone crazy! They see a sheep, and think it's a pig or a dog! And what's all this about it being an embarrassing offering?"

But angry as he was, he tried to control his emotions as he neared the temple, not wanting them to contaminate his offering. As he struggled to do this, another priest appeared before him and poked the sheep with his staff.

"Why on earth are you carrying this heavy elephant around? If you knew how to play a flute, you could ride the elephant, instead of walking with it on your back. Tsk, tsk."

The priest gave the man a pitying look, shaking his head as he left. All of this was just too strange for the man.

He set the sheep down and just stood there with his mouth open. He had been standing there for quite a while when his eyes suddenly became bright and he started chuckling.

"Ah, now I understand. There was no need to carry all this weight around. I was just causing myself unnecessary hardship!"

He looked at the sheep that he had carried with so much sweat and difficulty, then untied its legs. He let it go, and without even a backwards glance, he returned to his village.

※

We all are inherently endowed with our fundamental mind. Although people don't realize this, it's what has guided us through a billion years of evolution.

Unfortunately, as we've evolved, we gathered all kinds of habits and views, and these have become karmic states of consciousness that block our awareness of our fundamental mind. So instead of correctly seeing our true nature, our sight is distorted and we think we're seeing a pig, a dog, or an elephant. When we look at others, instead of truly seeing them, all we see is our own level of consciousness.

This is part of what the priests had been trying to teach the man, for each one could sense that the man was finally ready to understand this.

People have carried these heavy karmic burdens for so long that they've come to treasure them and don't want to put them down. However, if you think about it, even those karmic states of consciousness have come from your foundation, so what's more natural than setting them down and entrusting them to the place they came from? You'll feel so much lighter!

When you completely let go of the thoughts of "me" as well, your foundation will become clear to you, and you won't be misled by the things that arise.

Can you imagine how free you'll feel? This is what the priest meant by saying that the man could have been sitting on the elephant, playing a flute and riding it around.

Start where you are right now, with your thoughts, your speech, and your actions, and entrust them as they are to your foundation. Then, one by one, the record of what you've done in the past will be erased. It's recorded over, and a blank tape is all that's left.

The first step on this path is to let go of thoughts of "I." When you give something or help someone, pay close attention, and when you find yourself thinking "I did this or that," let go of those thoughts.

If you carry around these thoughts of "I did" and "I am," then no matter how great a donation you gave, no matter how hard you worked, your effort will never produce virtue and merit.

If you truly want to help someone, if you truly want to give something, then do it while entrusting everything to your foundation. Then, karmic consciousnesses won't be formed, and true virtue and merit will arise.

33. True Giving

One day, when the sunims were out collecting donations of food for their temple, one sunim entered the yard of a house that looked so poor he felt guilty about asking them for anything.

He had turned around and was leaving when the owner called out to him. His family had very little, but they wanted to make an offering.

Not having any food, this family had gone around asking people for the water they washed their rice in, which was normally just thrown away. They added a bit of rice to this water and boiled it down until it thickened a bit. Then they would drink it like a soup.

Using their best bowl and a serving table, the family offered a bowl of this rice water to the sunim, who humbly accepted it.

As the sunim drank it, he was moved to tears by their sincerity and wanted to do something to help them. He had nothing of his own to give, but he could find them some firewood. So, later in the day, he took up an empty pack and headed into the mountains. He collected all the wood he could carry and was on his way to their house when he met his teacher.

His teacher asked him what he was doing, and the sunim explained the whole story to him. As soon as the sunim finished, his teacher swung his staff around and started beating the sunim's legs mercilessly while roaring:

"What do you think you're doing? You're a sunim! For years now you've been studying this vast and profound fundamental mind! You should be helping them through formless giving! Once they've burnt up that wood, your help is gone! And you would call that giving?!"

The sunim rolled around on the ground, still wearing his pack load of firewood, clutching his calves, with tears streaming down his face. Finally he sat up and was wiping away his tears and blood when suddenly he understood formless giving.

"That's it! That's it!" Blood was still trickling down his leg, but now he understood the principle of entrusting a thought to his fundamental mind.

All of his pain and shock were forgotten, and he felt so light and free that he thought he might start flying. He took all of his gratitude and best wishes for the family and silently entrusted them to his foundation.

Before too long, the family that had given him the rice water began to flourish until eventually they became one of the most prosperous families in the village.

⁎⁎

The benefit of raising a good thought for someone and entrusting that to your fundamental mind can't be compared to the temporary help that material goods provide.

When you selflessly entrust a wish to help someone to your foundation, when you do this while letting go of any hint of "I'm doing" or "I did," then that help continues without ceasing. It never ends, and it helps them on a very fundamental level. Not only that, the virtue and merit of that act eventually returns to you.

Pay careful attention to the thoughts you're giving rise to. "I don't know anything," "I'm sick," "I don't have anything"—don't let statements like these guide your thinking, speech, or actions. Don't let them become excuses for thinking of only yourself.

If you do, the results will not be good. This is because all of your thoughts, words, and actions return to you. They are input into your foundation and then come back out with different appearances.

If you use your mind narrowly and shallowly, the poverty of that opens up before you. If you use your mind deeply and inclusively, peace and warmth lie as far as the eye can see.

Truly, a single thought can create heaven, and a single thought can create hell.

Other Books by Daehaeng Kun Sunim

- *Wake Up and Laugh*
- *No River to Cross*
- *A Thousand Hands of Compassion*
   [2010 iF communication design Award]
- *Touching the Earth* (forthcoming)
- *Moon in a Thousand Rivers* (forthcoming)
- *Practice in Daily Life* (Series, bilingual, Korean/English)
    1. To Discover Your True Self, "I" Must Die
    2. Walking Without a Trace
    3. Let Go and Observe
    4. Mind, Treasure House of Happiness
    5. The Furnace Within Yourself
    6. The Spark that Can Save the Universe
    7. The Infinite Power of One Mind
    8. Within the Heart of a Moment
    9. One with the Universe (forthcoming)
    10. Protecting the Earth (forthcoming)

Foreign language editions from Hanmaum Publications

- 건널 강이 어디 있으랴 (Korean)
- 내 마음은 금부처 (Korean)
- *El Camino Interior* (Spanish)
- *Vida de la Maestra Seon Daehaeng* (Spanish)
- *Enseñanzas de la Maestra Daehaeng* (Spanish)
- *Práctica del Seon en la vida diaria* (Colección)
    (bilingual, Spanish/English)
    1. Una semilla inherente alimenta el Universo

- *Si te lo propones, no hay imposibles* (Spanish)
- 人生不是苦海 (Traditional Chinese)
- 无河可渡 (Simplified Chinese)
- 我心是金佛 (Simplified Chinese) (Forthcoming 2014)

Foreign language editions from other publishers

- *Wie fließendes Wasser*
    Goldmann Arkana-Random House, Germany
- *Vertraue und Lass Alles Los*
    Goldmann Arkana-Random House, Germany
- *Umarmt von Mitgefühl*
    Diederichs-Random House, Germany
- *Wache auf und lache*
    Theseus, Germany
- *Ningún Río Que Cruzar*
    Kailas Editorial, S.L., Spain
- 我心是金佛
    Oak Tree Publishing Co., Taiwan
- *Дзэн и просветление*
    Amrita-Rus, Russia
- *Sup Cacing Tanah*
    PT Gramedia, Indonesia
- *Không có sông nào để vượt qua*
    Phuong Nam Books, Vietnam
- *No River to Cross* (title to be determined)
    Arabic edition of *No River to Cross*
    Sphinx Publishing, Egypt, Forthcoming 2014

Anyang Headquarters of Hanmaum Seonwon

(430-040) 101-62 Seoksu-dong, Manan-gu, Anyang-si
Gyeonggi-do, Republic of Korea
Tel: (82-31) 470-3175 / Fax: (82-31) 470-3209
www.hanmaum.org/eng
onemind@hanmaum.org

Overseas Branches of Hanmaum Seonwon

ARGENTINA
Buenos Aires
Miró 1575, CABA, C1406CVE, Rep. Argentina
Tel: (54-11) 4921-9286 / Fax: (54-11) 4921-9286
www.hanmaum.org.ar

Tucumán
Av. Aconquija 5250, El Corte, Yerba Buena,
Tucumán, T4107CHN, Rep. Argentina
Tel: (54-381) 425-1400
www.hanmaumtuc.org

BRASIL
Sao Paulo
R. Newton Prado 540, Bom Retiro
Sao Paulo, C.P 01127-000, Brasil
Tel: (55-11) 3337-5291
www.hanmaumbr.org

CANADA
Toronto
20 Mobile Dr., North York, Ontario M4A 1H9, Canada
Tel: (1-416) 750-7943 / Fax: (1-416) 981-7815
www.hanmaumcanada.org

GERMANY
Kaarst
Broicherdorf Str. 102, 41564 Kaarst, Germany
Tel: (49-2131) 969551 / Fax: (49-2131) 969552
www.hanmaum-zen.de

THAILAND
Bangkok
86-1 soi 4 Ekkamai Sukhumvit 63
Bangkok, Thailand
Tel: 070-8258-2391 / (66-2)391-0091
home.hanmaum.org/bangkok

USA
Chicago
7852 N. Lincoln Ave., Skokie, IL 60077, USA
Tel: (1-847) 674-0811
www.buddhapia.com/hmu/chi/

Los Angeles
1905 S. Victoria Ave., L.A., CA 90016, USA
Tel: (1-323) 766-1316
home.hanmaum.org/la

New York
144-39, 32 Ave., Flushing, NY 11354, USA
Tel: (1-718) 460-2019 / Fax: (1-718) 939-3974
www.juingong.org

Washington D.C.
7807 Trammel Rd., Annandale, VA 22003, USA
Tel: (1-703) 560-5166 / Fax: (1-703) 560-5566
http://home.hanmaum.org/wa

If you would like more information about these books or would like to order copies of them,
please call or write to:

Hanmaum International Culture Institute
Hanmaum Publications
101-60, Seoksu-dong, Manan-gu, Anyang-si
Gyeonggi-do, 430-040, Republic of Korea
Tel: (82-31) 470-3175
Fax: (82-31) 470-3209
e-mail: onemind@hanmaum.org

www.ingramcontent.com/pod-product-compliance
Lightning Source LLC
Chambersburg PA
CBHW032032040426
42449CB00007B/864